Financial Success

For

the Smiling Retiree BW

2nd Edition

Navi J. Dowty, CFA®

Copyright © 2019 Navi J. Dowty

All rights reserved.

No part of this book may be reproduced or transmitted in any form or by any means, electronic or mechanical, including photocopying, recording, or by any information storage and retrieval system, without permission in writing from the author.

First Printing 2019
First Edition 2019
9781798182239

Disclaimer

This book is presented solely for educational purposes and is not intended to represent or be used as an exhaustive financial resource. The information contained in this book is made available for illustrative purposes, explaining only the basics of investment planning.

The author emphasizes this material is not offered as financial, legal, accounting, or other professional services' advice. It is highly recommended you seek the services of a competent professional before making any decisions regarding your business or personal finances.

Best efforts have underscored the writing of this book, but the author and publisher make no representations or warranties of any kind and assume no liabilities of any kind with respect to the accuracy or completeness of the contents, and specifically disclaim any implied warranties of use for any particular purpose.

The author, shall not be held liable or responsible to any person or entity with respect to any loss or incidental or consequential damages caused, or alleged to have been caused, directly or indirectly, by the information contained in this book, or disruption caused by errors or omissions, whether such errors or omissions result from negligence, accident, or any other cause.

The case studies and any references are fictional, and any likeness to actual persons, either living or dead, is completely coincidental. The investment case studies represented in this book were created to show only the highlights of how an investor might choose to make investment decisions.

The reader is advised to consult with a professional financial advisor who has experience with guiding clients and making investment choices relevant to an individual's financial situation.

Dedication

This book is dedicated to:

The memory of my grandparents James and Bernice Barnhart who always believed in me and inspired me to take on ever bigger challenges.

The memory of my father, IvanDowty, who taught me the value of hard work.

The memory of my mother, Mary Jeanne Dowty who taught me the value of education.

I further dedicate this book to all of the financial educators and other professionals with whom we have collaborated with over the years so that we have been able to continually improve the services that we can provide to our deserving and faithful clients.

To my many loyal clients without whom, I have had the opportunity and privilege to work with in becoming Smiling Retirees

And most of all, to my precious wife Susan Dowty, my love, my best friend and my inspiration. And God's perfect partner for me who makes our life worthwhile.

About The Author

Navi J. Dowty, CFA®

Navi J. Dowty, CFA is a Financial Educator, Best Selling Author, and Retirement Income Planning Specialist, who has earned the prestigious Chartered Financial Analyst designation, which is the worlds most respected investment professional's achievement. It is held by less than 1% and not held by 99% of financial advoisors. Navi (pronounced Navy) has shared his professional insights in multiple publications, including Forbes magazine, Elite Advisor, Business ICONS, and the Daily Herald, and the bestselling financial books, Your Dream Retirement, and Batsocks, Vegas and Conservative Investing as well as at the Leadership Speakers Academy at West Point, sharing the main stage recently with the Legendary Astronaut, Buzz Aldrin.

He has been invited to share his insights at the Harvard Business Experts Forum, The Harvard Expert Story Tellers Conference, and NASDAQ. He is the author of the Best Selling Book, *Financial Success For the Smiling Retiree*, as well as *Tax Secrets for the Smiling Retiree*, and *Income Secrets For The Smiling Retiree*.

He has been interviewed on radio and TV, ABC, and CBS as well as radio. He has taught continuing education for other financial professionals as well as acted as an expert witness.

Among his many other charitable activities, Navi sponsored and mentored a high school team at the U.S. First Robot contest, to help high school students develop an interest in science and engineering. This endeavor resulted in them winning the prestigious Motorola Quality Award.

As the Creator of *The Smiling Retiree Process*, Navi has been a financial consultant to individuals and corporations for over 45 years (creating *"smiling retirees"*). Navi specializes in increasing income and reducing taxes for retirees, executives, entrepreneurs, women on their own, and corporations, along with preserving their assets from wealth "predators."

He has a gift for helping others develop their financial decision-making skills.

Navi is the Founder and CEO of Navi Dowty Associates, Inc., DuPage Tax Group, Inc. and Associated Retirement Planners, Inc., a Registered Investment Advisor.

This Book is for You

…if you are near retirement or in retirement now and you want to know how to:

- Optimize your wealth
- Increase your income
- Avoid high taxes
- Stay ahead of inflation
- Use interest rates to your advantage

This book reveals some of the investment secrets every *Smiling Retiree* needs to know!

NAVI DOWTY & ASSOCIATES, INC.
ASSOCIATED RETIREMENT PLANNERS, INC.

Associated Retirement Planners, Inc. is a Registered Investment Advisory Firm. Investments are offered thru Associated Retirement Planners, Inc.

Returns sited are just hypothetical examples and are not guaranteed.

Navi Dowty & Associates, Inc.

Associated Retirement Planners, Inc.

290 S. County Farm Rd, Ste P

Wheaton, IL 60187

(630) 893-4142

And

1102 Grand Avenue

Wausau, Wisconsin 54403

(715) 845-4367

www.NaviDowty.com

Acknowledgments

I wish to personally thank the following people for their help with creating this book:

All of the many Navi Dowty & Associates, Inc. and Associated Retirement Planners, Inc. valued clients; thank you for your trust throughout the years.

And best of all, Susan R. Dowty, for your illustrations, of course, but mostly for your love.

Foreword

With a book like this, there is always a trade-off. Do you write it technically, so it is mathematically correct for the academics? Or do you make it more general and more accessible to the general public? I have chosen to make this a more general and descriptive book with some ideas and a minimum of graphs and equations. As I go through the many edits, I also find that I am repeating myself in various places. If it drives the reader crazy, I understand. It drives me crazy, too, but some people will use this to reference different ideas by simply looking in the table of contents and going to a particular section. The great themes of this book are to try to protect yourself from rising taxes, interest rates, and inflation and don't lose money. These affect every area, and so I find myself saying, "If David Walker is right and tax rates double," in many places. I have to repeat this because if you just look at one section, I can't assume that you read the other section about rising taxes. It will affect everything, so please bear with the repetition.

I watched my grandparents go from being very prosperous when they retired to virtual destitution in their later years. They followed all of the rules that people were told… Work hard. Save your money. They did that. My grandfather was the chief engineer at a paper company. He was pretty much an electrical genius. He built the big power generators and paper machines. He could fix anything. But after he retired, inflation started, and then when he died, my grandmother lived on the ever-diminishing purchasing power of her fixed income. They did not count on inflation. Why would they? All their lives, the job of the Federal Reserve was to protect the value of the dollar. That all changed and they weren't equipped to change with it.

When I was on a trip at age 12, visiting my grandparents in Los Angeles, I was robbed at knifepoint in the science museum.

These two events formed the basis of my thinking and approach to taking care of my clients. I vowed that I would not let them be taken advantage of.

The main focus of this book is how to get enough net retirement income to fund your lifestyle in retirement. It looks to me like, for the vast majority of Americans, providing for an adequate income in retirement is by far the most critical strategy needed. I observed long ago that most people

approaching retirement do not have a clear vision of how they want their life to look in the future or a plan of how to get there.

If I asked 1,000 people what their plan is, it is basically "We hope the market keeps going up." A small percentage of Americans have so much money that income is of no concern, but for the vast majority of people approaching retirement, the most vital questions are, "How do I get enough income after taxes and after inflation to fund my lifestyle in retirement?"

For most Americans approaching retirement, most of their money is invested in their retirement accounts in the stock market. When we are just starting out, wide fluctuations in prices help us accumulate money faster. Unfortunately, in retirement, while withdrawing money from your retirement accounts, those same fluctuations can make the accounts go down faster. The other thing almost nobody is talking about is the sequence of withdrawals. Should we use our retirement accounts first, or our Social Security, or our after-tax brokerage accounts, or our tax-free Roths? What happens when taxes, interest rates, and inflation go up? Not if…but when.

We can only get five benefits out of an investment portfolio. We can get growth, income, liquidity, tax benefits or detriments, and some level of protection or risk. You need to pick what is most important to you, understanding that there will be tradeoffs.

These are some of the fundamental questions that need to be answered to properly plan to become *Smiling Retirees.*

Table Of Contents

About The Author i
Foreword vii
Chapter 1 1
Questions People Ask 1
Question #1: Can I retire yet? 1
Question #2: How can I make more money? 3
Question #3: Do I have my money in the right place? 5
Question #4: How much risk should I be taking? 8
Question #5: How much money do I have to save so I can retire? 9
Question #6: When should I start Social Security? 12
Question #7: Should I take the pension buyout? 14
Question #8: How do I save on paying taxes? 18
Question #10: How do I own real estate in my IRA? 26
Question #11: How much money can I give to my kids? 27
Question #12: Do I really have to pay taxes after 70 years of age? 28
Question #13. What about gold, real estate, bitcoins, and ETFs? 30
Question #14. Can I make IRA contributions after 70½? 33
Chapter 2 36
Questions People Should Be Asking…But Are Not! 36
Question #1: How do I get enough net income to fund my lifestyle in retirement? 36
Question #2: Who should I be dealing with? 40
Question #3: What is a good investment strategy? 42

Question #4: Should I try to get most of my money into the tax-free category? If so, how? 44

Question #5: How do I plan for someone to take care of me later in retirement if I need help? 47

Question #6: How do I fund my health care if I need help? 50

Question #7: Should we live in our current home until retirement? 51

Question #8: What happens to my retirement lifestyle if a black swan event occurs?...53

Question #9: What if I convert to a Roth IRA and the rules change, increasing the tax on my future withdrawals?..58

Question #10: The company I'm investing in…is it risky? 60

Question #11: How do I know if my advisor and I are compatible?........62

Chapter 3 68

Inaccurate Beliefs People Have About Investing 68

Myth #1: The market has returned 6% so I'll be okay if I take out 4%...68

Myth #2: The Stock Market (Mutual Funds) Is the Only Place for My Money. 73

Myth #3: If I Shift Money Out of My Retirement Account, I Will Pay Taxes. 77

Myth #4: I should defer income taxes on my retirement monies as long as possible. 80

Myth #5: My income needs will be lower in retirement, so I can live on 75% of what I'm living on now. 87

Myth #6: My taxes will be lower in retirement...89

Myth #7: Corporate earnings tell the story of the health of a company..91

Myth #8: Published percentage returns show the effect of an investment's ability to make money for me. 93

Myth #9: Bonds are safe investments. 95

Myth #10: The best place for my 401(k) is with my old employer.........98

Chapter 4 101
Techniques people could be using but are not. 101
Technique #1: Shifting funds to tax-advantaged investments. 101
Technique #2: Creating income from your stocks. 104
Technique #3: Selling real estate (or highly appreciated stocks) without paying tax on the gain. 109
Technique #4: Creating family and tax-friendly entities to create more income. 112
Technique #5: Sell at the top, buy at the bottom. 115
Technique #6: Diversify into different non-correlated assets. 117
Technique #7: Calculate the effect of various financial maneuvers. 120
Technique #8: Seeing what the corporate insiders are doing. 122
Technique #9: Build a good financial team. 124

Chapter 5 126
Fundamental Mistakes You Might Be Making 126
Mistake #1: Not switching from accumulation to preservation at the right time. 126
Mistake #2: Having all your money in one asset category. 131
Mistake #3: Relying on statistics or market returns to manage your retirement funds. 135
Mistake #4: Relying on withdrawals from your retirement accounts to fund your retirement. 143
Mistake #5: Not taking income taxes into account. 145
Mistake #6: Not taking inflation into account 146
Mistake #7: Not taking rising interest rates into account. 147
Mistake #8: Ignoring the Buffet rule: Don't lose money 149
Mistake #9: Not taking the sequence of returns into account. 151
Mistake #10: Not taking the sequence of withdrawals into account.

.... 152
Mistake #11: Not using charitable strategies.............................. 153
Mistake #12: Judging items by their name rather than by what they actually do. 153
Mistake #13: Confusing correlation with causation.............................. 157
Mistake #14: Not evaluating "What if I'm wrong?"........................... 161
Appendix 164

Chapter 1
QUESTIONS PEOPLE ASK

This section of the book answers some of the most common questions asked by retirees, or people who are about to become retirees. Most of these questions can be answered precisely only when based on your unique circumstances. As everyone's personal financial situation varies, it is always a wise choice to meet with a professional financial advisor with years of market experience and the ability to recommend a variety of options that may serve your particular situation and financial needs.

Question #1: Can I retire yet?

Everyone wants to know the answer to this question, and it depends on your view of the future. How much money do you need now, every month? Will you spend less in retirement? Probably not. Most people are unable to cut back when they retire …and may even need more money then.

Some folks put off doing the things they want to do until they retire, like traveling and seeing all of the places that you have been dreaming about visiting. If you think that you will spend less in retirement, are you going to skip those things that you have been putting off, and even cut out some of the things that you are now doing? You'll need to figure out your costs, and then plan on rising costs. If you are factoring a 3% per year increase in the cost of living, you may be under-budgeting. You probably should factor in rising income taxes also, as there seems to be a new trend developing.

As an example, let's say you need $100,000 per year right now to live the lifestyle you want. If so, you probably need $125,000 before taxes, depending on where you live, and your state and local taxes, your deductions, and your filing status. These are rough numbers used to illustrate the point. If inflation is 4% per year, in 10 years you will need $184,706 instead of the $125,000 in your first year of retirement. In 20 years you'll need $273,086, which is more than double what you need in the first year.

If inflation and tax increases are higher, you'll need even more income. Subtract Social Security and any other fixed income sources you have, such as a pension, or annuity income. What's left is your net income need. You can't count on working forever because there will come a time when you simply can't work. This income needs to come from one, or more of these four sources: interest, dividends, rents or royalties and NOT from simply selling off shares of your mutual funds, in your retirement accounts. That's the fast road to insolvency.

So here's a question for you: Have you accumulated enough so that your assets will produce that amount of growing, after-tax income, and have at least six months to a year of spending, set aside for an emergency fund? If so, you probably have enough to retire as a Smiling Retiree.

> "October: This is one of the particularly dangerous months to invest in stocks. Other dangerous months are July, January, September, April, November, May, March, June, December, August, and February."
>
> Mark Twain
> (He is right, Navi Dowty)

Question #2: How can I make more money?

When I hear this question, I assume it means the person asking the question wants more income. As I mentioned in answer to the first question, there are only four real sources of income, besides going back to work, and they are:

1. Interest
2. Dividends
3. Rents
4. Royalties

People may think that getting monthly income by selling off their mutual funds in their retirement accounts is income, but it's not. Usually, people are hoping that the value of what they retain will go up enough to replace the value of what they sold. This is unrealistic. It works sometimes, but you can't count on it.

Think of the farmer on the edge of town who retires and sells an acre or two to someone who wants to build a house. It's possible that real estate values go up and the farmer feels like he or she still has as much left as when they started. The farmer can do this a few more times, but eventually, all the land is gone. Sometimes real estate prices go down, and almost nothing is left. I often tell this story, and it surprises me how many people knew someone who experienced this.

To figure out your income needs, first, you need to think of how much money you need immediately available. This is called "liquid money," or "emergency money." The rest of your assets you can invest for a longer period with the hope of making more return. If you choose to invest, there are only five fundamental categories: stocks, bonds, real estate, cash, and commodities. Everything else is some combination or derivative of these five fundamental categories.

Mutual funds, for example, are composed of stocks or bonds.

REITs (real estate investment trusts) are investments in real estate. Annuities, the fixed variety, are cash accounts with insurance companies and are somewhat similar to the CDs offered by banks, but without the FDIC Insurance. All of these require you to invest your money for longer than your savings or checking accounts, and while they may have more risk, the Smiling Retiree knows they all have the potential to make you more money.

Question #3: Do I have my money in the right place?

This is a great question, and the answer depends on which of the following five benefits you want to accomplish:

- Growth
- Income
- Liquidity
- Tax benefits
- Some degree of safety or protection

Can you think of any other characteristics of an investment? There really aren't any, so you have to choose what is important to you. We want all of these, don't we? I know I do, but there's a problem. When you choose one, you diminish the effect of the others. The more growth you want, the less protection you have, and probably less income as well. Let's approach this topic by looking at it from the perspective of an investor's stage of life.

In general, if you're just starting out, your financial task is to accumulate investment assets. This means you would emphasize growth. If you're, let's say, within five years of retirement, you'll want to emphasize more preservation. You can look at your overall investment mix and ask yourself, "How much of this can I afford to lose?" You have to be realistic! If you're 25, you might not like it if your account goes down and loses value, but it won't hurt you in the long run, and probably will even help you. This is because you're probably putting money into your retirement account every month. We call this "dollar-cost averaging," and it's one of the best accumulation strategies there is, assuming you have enough time. Of course, this works in reverse when you're taking money out of your account to support your lifestyle in retirement. Your account may go down faster with fluctuating prices when you are withdrawing money.

Cash in its many forms and bonds are regarded more as preservation vehicles while stocks, real estate, and commodities are viewed as growth strategies and, as always, there are exceptions. If you use bonds, be sure that they are issued by pretty conservative entities. U. S Government bonds for example. Or maybe a household name consumer company that you see every day at the mall. Of course, you have to be satisfied with the yield and duration on the bonds. Very short term bonds will fluctuate less in price with changing interest rates than longer-term bonds. As you get closer to retirement, you should probably tilt your investments more toward preserving your hard-earned money once you've accumulated enough to live comfortably for the rest of your life. Whatever you do, don't lose it! And by the way, don't fall for the idea that the market will always come back. Many of those 'dot com' companies that people flooded into in the late '90s don't exist anymore. They are not coming back. Smiling Retirees choose their investments carefully and consider getting the advice of an experienced professional.

> "The stocks have reached what looks like a permanently high plateau."
> Professor Irving Fisher, Fall of 1929
>
> (He was off a little, Navi Dowty)

Question #4: How much risk should I be taking?

That's the fundamental question, isn't it? You should certainly be taking more risk if you are trying to accumulate money, and less if you're trying to preserve it. Not too helpful? Here is an old rule of thumb: Take 100 and subtract your age. That is the highest percentage of your money you should have at risk. If you're 65, you would want to have, at the most, 35% of your money at risk. This is a very rough guideline, though. Maybe you have a lot of money and are living off your rents, interest, dividends or royalties. If so, then it may not matter if the current value of your wealth drops for a year or longer. As long as you have enough income, you will probably be all right.

The vast majority of Americans, however, have most of their wealth tied up in the stock market in retirement accounts, and they plan to simply withdraw money every month after they retire. In other words, they will be practicing reverse dollar-cost averaging. If you are in this situation, it matters vitally if the account value drops as it has in past declines. It doesn't matter that it may come back if you've taken out money after it went down. If it drops in half, and you're taking out 4% of the pre-drop value, your next withdrawal will be at the rate of 8% of the previous value. In other words, your account may disappear faster.

If you're going to be living in retirement by withdrawing your money from your accounts, you must shift at least some of your money into more protection. Move your money into protected accounts such as very short term Treasuries, fixed annuities, CDs, and some cash accounts, so you reduce your risk. Smiling Retirees pick whichever ones are paying the most at the time and go with that.

The real question is: "How do you manage the right amount of risk so you get what you want and need in retirement?"

Question #5: How much money do I have to save so I can retire?

Probably a lot more than you first thought. As discussed in the first question **"Can I retire yet?"**, You need enough to provide the lifestyle you want in retirement after taking into account rising living costs and probable rising income taxes. David Walker, the former controller general of the U.S. government, told Congress in 2008 they would have to double taxes to make ends meet. If he's right, we will have higher future income taxes.

Some tax saving strategies may hurt you if tax rates go down, but we are actually very near the all-time low in tax brackets. The effect of taxes on your future income can require complex calculations because you need to figure both rising costs and rising taxes and make a guess at what your future earnings will be as well. This can be done in a spreadsheet, or you can find a good financial advisor to do it for you.

The big problem is that you have to make some assumptions. If you just take an average return that you think your accounts might earn, you will probably be misled. The online calculators where you input how much you now have, how much you need, and how much you will earn completely miss the point of rising taxes and costs, and more importantly, miss the probability that returns will likely be negative in some years while you're withdrawing from your accounts. This can make your accounts deplete even faster. Maybe interest rates will rise enough so bank accounts will again pay a livable interest rate, but you can't go into retirement banking on hope. You need to base your decisions on facts. Even if interest rates go back up, inflation will most likely go up even faster.

To give you some idea, if you have $1 million saved and you're 65 years old, you can withdraw $28,571 per year for the next 35 years if you earn 0 percent interest. If the $1 million is in your retirement account and you will have to pay 20% of it in taxes on the income, the amount you have after taxes is $22,857. If this is taxable, it may also trigger taxation on your social security, further reducing the net amount you have to spend.

Let's assume for a minute that you've planned ahead and the $1 million is in a tax-free account such as a Roth IRA. If you can earn 4%, you can withdraw $53,577 per year. Add that to your other income such as social security, and maybe a pension, and you can live pretty well in most parts of the country in today's dollars. However, costs will probably go up. If inflation is only 3%, your actual purchasing power will be reduced to $34,003 after taxes and inflation, and you can try to live on that annual sum for the next 35 years and run out of money at age 100. If inflation is higher than 3%, it will eat into your nest egg even faster.

If you use the Rule of 72, you can divide any rate of return into 72 and calculate roughly how many years it takes for the figure to double, like this: 72 / 3 equals 24. At only 3% inflation, your costs double in 24 years if costs rise by 6% per year, its only 12 years before your costs double. (For the scientists and engineers reading this, I know the actual number is 69.3147, but we round it up to 72 so that it is easier to estimate in your head. Remember, it is only an estimate). Obviously you can see that you may need more than $1 million saved up, after taxes, to retire. Or, you may need income sources that can go up with rising costs, such as rental income. Smiling Retirees know it's a balancing act, and this is the art of retirement income planning. You have to balance your risk against your income needs.

Question #6: When should I start Social Security?

This is yet another trade-off. As I'm writing this, every year you delay taking social security past your full retirement age will give you 8% more income, simple interest.

Like many of these tips, it is a calculation with many moving parts. Experts tell us there are over 500 ways a couple can take their social security payments. The big idea, though, is that if you need the income now, take it. If you don't need the income, delay it. In fact, you might want to consider subjecting your tax-deferred accounts to tax now, if you believe that tax rates will be higher in the future. In other words, spend some of your IRA or 401k money first, delaying social security until age 70. At present, there is no reason to delay beyond age 70.

Can you take half of your older spouse's social security at 62 and let your social security grow until full retirement age? No, you can't do that. If you start social security before full retirement age, the system will start yours and just add enough of your spouse's to make up the difference, meaning that your social security account stops growing from delayed credits. It can still grow from your contributions. If you start early, you will always receive less per year.

There are classes all over the country about how to maximize social security. You might need to talk to someone who has the social security maximization software to make these calculations for you. But remember, social security is just one pillar of your retirement income. Smiling Retirees need to figure how it all fits together, kind of like the teeth on a ~~house~~ key: if any of the teeth are off just a little, the key won't work!

Question #7: Should I take the pension buyout?

Like everything else, it's really just a calculation. People come in and ask, "Should I take $4,238 a month, or instead take the whole $1,000,000 in my pension account?"

You'll have to decide which choice is best for you.

Sometimes the numbers are so great on the monthly income side that you can't beat it. The problem with taking a monthly pension, though, is that once you take it, it's inflexible. You have to take it for the rest of your life, or for the rest of your life and your spouse's life. Remember, though, that pension payments end on your, or yours and your spouse's, death. Nothing is left for your heirs. What happens if you get run over by a truck a year after you start your pension? It is gone.

A pension means you'll be receiving funds for life like your parents and grandparents probably had when they retired. The auto workers in Detroit got pensions; government employees get pensions…they get a monthly check. Of course, the payout will be less if you receive income for two lives, and you can't leave any pension funds to your kids.

Once you die, the pension payments are gone, too. While you're alive, you can't stop the monthly payments, and if you need more money you can't call up and say, "I need $50,000; send it to me". If you win the lottery one year and you don't need any pension, you can't stop the payments. The payments keep coming, and that's why I say it's inflexible.

On the other hand, if the company says, "Instead of sending you $4,238 a month, we'll give you the full lump sum of $1,000,000," then you have to make some careful calculations. Can you replace your monthly income by taking the lump sum and creating your own "private pension"? Can you take some of the income from your private pension and insure yourself, and still have money left over every month? These are all calculations you have to do to make this decision. I can't do them for you in this book because I don't know what your numbers from your company will be.

The advantage of receiving the full lump sum, of course, is that now you have flexibility, but only if the numbers work out right. Depending on how you set up your private pension, you can start your disbursements. You can stop them, too. If you need more money, you can reach in and take some out, and if you die along the way, your heirs can receive the balance.

So that's the question: "Can you replace your monthly income by taking the lump sum and investing it properly?"

I can't say if you should do it or not do it because I don't know your individual situation without getting together and carefully going over your personal circumstances. Sometimes you want to retire, but you don't need to take any income right away.

So typically, when people ask, "Should I take the pension or the buyout?" they're getting ready to retire. Let's say you are 65 and you have to make a decision. You may not want more income. Maybe you're already in a high tax bracket, or maybe your spouse is still working, and the extra income from the pension pushes you into a higher tax bracket or causes tax on your social security. You may want to delay taking that income and increase your flexibility by taking the buyout, assuming that the numbers work out. Another benefit of taking the buyout is that you don't have the risk of the company going out of business or having financial problems and being unable to pay the pension. Think of Harrisburg, PA, Detroit, MI, the steel companies, or the airline companies where people lost their pensions because of financial difficulty or even bankruptcy.

Bottom line, Smiling Retirees get out their calculators or consult with a financial advisor well versed in making these judgments, so they can tell which choice is the best one for their financial circumstances. Smiling Retirees don't guess!

> **An investment in knowledge pays the best interest.**
>
> **Benjamin Franklin**

Question #8: How do I save on paying taxes?

We're talking about income taxes. We could talk about all kinds of taxes, but if I asked the question, "What's the biggest expense in your entire lifetime?" what will people say? Most people would say it's their house or medical expenses, but far and away the biggest expense will almost always be the money you pay in income tax. This is true even today when we're near the lowest tax rates ever in modern history.

So how can you save on paying your income tax? People approaching retirement are really asking, "How can I save tax on my earnings or retirement account withdrawals?" Also, most people don't know there's a ticking tax time bomb for everyone who has a retirement account, which I'll get to in a minute.

Think of your money in three different piles:

1. Tax now

2. Tax later

3. Tax never

The "tax now" money is going to be money that earns interest or dividends, or maybe rental income, right now, today. Like a savings account. You have to pay taxes on the earnings every year, even if you don't take anything out of the account.

The "tax later" accounts are all your retirement accounts,

annuities, and other investments where the tax is deferred until you actually take it out.

The "tax never" (sometimes called the tax-advantaged) would be withdrawals from Roth IRAs, Roth 401(k)s, Roth 403(b)s, or loans from life insurance cash value policies. So how do you save taxes?

Here's an important tip. All your life it has been to your advantage to delay paying tax on your retirement money. Let's say you put money into a retirement account when your tax rate was 50% and you can withdraw it later at the 35% rate. You delayed the tax, and you've taken it out at a lower bracket, which is a tremendous benefit, and this has been true in everyone's lifetime, until 2013, when the top tax brackets started going up. The highest income tax rates in our country occurred in the last two years of World War II when the top tax bracket was 94%. If you look at the '70s, it was high then, too, at 70%.

Top Tax Brackets

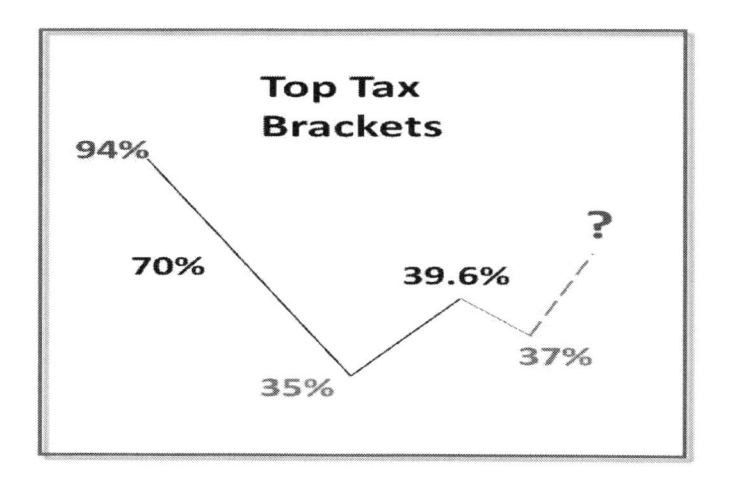

94%
70%
39.6%
35%
37%
?

In 2012 the top income tax bracket was 35%, but now tax rates have turned a corner and are beginning to go back up. The top bracket as I'm writing this is 37%. While it has paid to delay paying income taxes all your life, this may no longer be true!

There are actually all kinds of ways to save on income taxes, and here are a few ideas to consider.

One idea is to shift money from your "tax now" (taxable) accounts to your "tax-later" accounts (tax deferred), or to your "tax-never" (tax-free, or as some people call them, tax-advantaged) accounts.

Should you do that? Maybe. Again, it depends on your circumstances and some careful calculations, taking your future needs into account as well as the future cost of inflation, and probable future income tax increases. The way I like to do it is to try to shift your accounts fast enough to get you out of the worst of the tax time-bomb phase while keeping you in the same tax bracket. In other words, as I'm writing this, a couple with a taxable income of $78,950 and less (but above $19,400) will be in the 12% tax bracket for federal taxes.

If you have more than $78.950 in taxable income (line 10 on your tax return), you'll then go into the 22% or 24% tax bracket. You could go all the way up to $321,450 and stay in the 24% tax bracket (for a married couple filing jointly). By the time you read this, of course, the details will be different, but the principle remains the same... If your taxable income is above the 32% tax bracket, you might want to use some other tax saving strategies.

Subjecting this money to taxation now, and not later as we've all been taught to think, could be a smart move because federal taxes will probably be higher in the future. So this is one of the ways to save taxes on withdrawals you make in years to come.

There is something else important to consider. If you think about it, the money in your retirement account is not really all yours. Smiling Retirees know that the only way to really know how much of that money is theirs is when they can predict what the tax rates will be, and what tax bracket they'll be in, in the year they withdraw the money, and in all the years that follow.

You don't really know how much of that money in your retirement accounts is yours. You might say you have a million dollars in your accounts, but at a 30% taxation level, you really only receive 70% of that money. It could be even worse because your distributions may cause tax on your social security at the highest bracket, as well as pushing you into a higher tax bracket. If you have a $500,000 house with a $150,000 mortgage, you put $350,000 on your net worth statement because that is the net equity in your house. People don't do that with their retirement accounts because they pretend that all that money is theirs, but it really isn't. Part of it belongs to Uncle Sam. He is your partner, and he can change the rules every year.

And unlike the mortgage on your house which goes down every year that you are paying on it, the tax obligation on your retirement accounts get bigger as they grow in value. That is why we call this the ticking tax time bomb.

This is an example of how a good financial advisor can look at your unique situation and help guide you toward making the right decision, with a serious eye focused on the unknowns of the future.

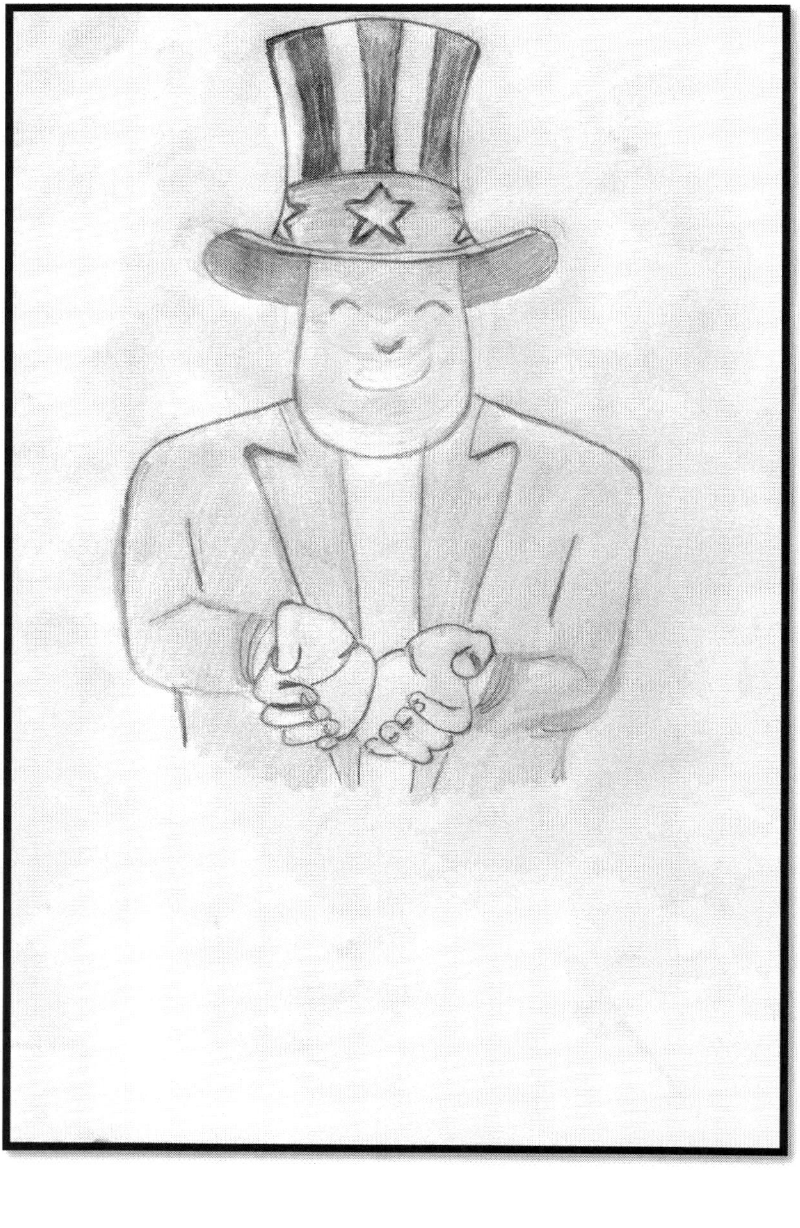

Financial Success: For the Smiling Retiree

Question #10: How do I own real estate in my IRA?

This is not something I would normally advise, but I'd make an exception if the only money you have to invest is in your retirement accounts.

If you wanted to buy a building or want to own real estate through your retirement account, how could you do that? First of all, you would have to have a self-directed IRA and have your account registered with a custodian that accepts real estate investments. You'd have to be very careful with any arrangements you make because the IRS has a lot of provisions you'd need to follow.

Section 408 of the Internal Revenue Code does not prohibit holding real estate in an IRA, assuming the transaction is not prevented by Section 4975 (prohibited transactions). You can't use the real estate yourself or for any family member. Of course, you cannot use your IRA funds to either purchase your home or vacation home, and there are other restrictions as well, or you could wind up with hefty taxes and penalties. If this is a topic of interest for you, I recommend consulting a tax specialist and having him or her work with your financial advisor.

One reason I'm skeptical about the value of this strategy is that you may find yourself increasing your taxes because the real estate may be taxed as capital gains outside your IRA, but when you take it out, you will be taxed at the higher ordinary income rate. You would have converted the lowest tax rate asset to the highest tax rate. It's important to select the right vehicle for your investments unless you want to get slammed by taxes.

People ask me this question, and I don't think it's a great idea. Tax-wise, it's horrible. Of course, Smiling Retirees know there are always exceptions, and under the right circumstances, buying real estate in your IRA could be right for you.

Question #11: How much money can I give to my kids?

When people ask this question, they're usually thinking of the gift tax, and the gift tax ceiling for 2019 is $15,000. When you read this, check what the current limit is. It may be higher in the future. A husband and wife can each give $15,000 to as many people as they wish, meaning a husband and wife could give $30,000 to each of their children and grandchildren without any gift tax implications. They can do this every year, and also they also have an $11.4 million lifetime exemption for the estate tax, right now. This will almost certainly change in the future, so check on the current rates. Be careful when giving appreciated assets like real estate or stocks. Your cost basis will carry over for tax purposes, and your kids will have to pay the income taxes on the gains. It may be better for them to inherit appreciated assets, so the taxable gain pain goes away.

Remember that different states have different rules, so you'd better check on this with a qualified tax professional in the state that you live before making any decisions. Any gifting that exceeds the $15,000 ceiling will eat into your lifetime exemption. Also, remember that the gift and estate tax and the income tax system are different. You may have to pay both or one or neither, depending on how you arrange things.

I don't know if it's a great idea to give massive amounts of money to our children…that's a whole different question. Warren Buffett has something to say about this. His comment is classic: he wants to give his kids "…*enough money so that they would feel they could do anything, but not so much that they could do nothing.*"

Smiling Retirees think that's good prudent advice.

Question #12: Do I really have to pay taxes after 70 years of age?

Yes, you do. The rule is that **whenEVER** you have taxable income, you have to pay tax.

Sometimes people are really asking, "Will my retirement monies be taxed?" They're thinking they've saved and invested all their life and built a nice nest egg and…now they're wondering if they are going to be taxed again. You will be taxed, and not just your retirement money but perhaps also your

Social Security.

Calculate this: if a couple's modified adjusted gross income, added to half of their Social Security payments, is over $44,000, they will have to pay tax on 85% percent of their social security…or, if the total is under $32,000, they have to pay tax on none of their Social Security. Between $32,000 and $44,000, they will pay tax on 50% of their Social Security.

By modified adjusted gross income I'm referring to the bottom number on the front page of the tax return, your adjusted gross income, and then adding back deductions for retirement accounts, and tax-exempt municipal bond interest. When you add one half of your Social Security income to your Modified Adjusted Gross Income, this number is called the Provisional Income.

This is one of the big reasons why *Smiling Retirees* know that municipal bond interest isn't really truly totally tax-free.

Question #13. What about gold, real estate, bitcoins, and ETFs?

> **The winds and the waves are always on the side of the ablest navigators.**
>
> **Edward Gibbon**

People are curious, and they want to know if they should put money into these different investment vehicles. I spoke with three people last month who asked me about bitcoins. What about ETFs? What about gold?

When folks ask about gold, what they're really asking is if they should purchase gold coins and stash them under their mattress or in a safe deposit box. Advertisements on TV or on the radio often suggest that people should buy gold. Frankly, when you hear those advertisements to buy gold, it's probably not the best time to buy gold because whenever anything is heavily promoted, it might be approaching a short term peak. Unfortunately, people usually buy at the top and sell at the bottom. That's why dollar-cost averaging is such a great strategy for most people, so you don't buy everything at the top and sell everything at the bottom.

But that's beside the point.

Here's my take on investing in gold, bitcoins, real estate, etc.

There are really only five things you can put your money into:

1. Stocks
2. Real estate
3. Bonds
4. Some form of cash accounts
5. Commodities

You could add things like collectables, crypto currencies or other currencies for that matter. But almost all of the money is in the above 5 categories.

All of these investments can have a place in your investment portfolio. The art of constructing a portfolio is simply figuring out how to put all these different elements together in a way that provides you with either growth, security, income, liquidity, tax benefits, or some desirable combination of them all.

The real question is how much of each category should you have? Could you have 5% of your money in gold? Of course, you could. Should you put all of your money in gold? Of course not. That would be silly. The question is really a matter of how much, not if, you should have in any of these categories.

When it comes to commodities, should you own gold stocks? Maybe not. Gold coins? Sure, why not? Diamonds, platinum, palladium, silver…yes, these commodities have value and could be stored in your safe deposit box. Why not? Why wouldn't you? You can think of gold as another type of currency. Diamonds would be a collectible that historically has kept up with inflation pretty well, as has gold and silver.

Is there a downside? Of course, there's a downside to everything. With bitcoins and ETFs, their liquidity depends on the Internet working. With real estate, you have to have an eager buyer if you are trying to sell. It is not liquid. I'm not saying it's a bad idea to have these different forms of value, just that you need to be judicious when developing your strategy.

Could you have 2% of your money in these different categories? 5%? 1%? If you have $2 million and you put 1% in bitcoins, you may have made a reasonable allocation. Could you have $20,000 in bitcoins? In gold coins? In diamonds? Sure, why not? It all depends on the context and the degree.

Should you have an ETF? Sure…have these if you wish…you'll usually have much lower fees than in the similar mutual fund. An ETF, or exchange-traded fund, is usually a single fund, traded on a stock exchange, like a stock, that tracks an index. You won't have the all-star fund manager, though. Real estate and ETFs can produce income. The others are like commodities, and you will only make money if they go up in value.

Smiling Retirees know that all of these investment vehicles could be good for their portfolio, but only if they know what they are, know their upside and downside, and they serve the overall investment strategy for growth, security, diversification, liquidity, and income.

So…why not?

> "It ain't what you don't know that gets you into trouble.
> It's what you know for sure that just ain't so."
>
> Mark Twain

Question #14. Can I make IRA contributions after 70½?

After age 70½, you can only make retirement plan contributions, like a 401(k), or a Roth IRA, if you, or your spouse, are still working. You cannot make any IRA deductible contributions after age 70½.

Even though you could contribute to a Roth IRA, you still have to begin taking money out of all your retirement accounts at 70½, except for your Roth IRA's. An important detail you need to know is that if you have retirement accounts in different categories, such as an IRA, a 401(k), a 457 plan, or a Keogh plan, you have to annually withdraw money from EACH of those categories.

The calculation is one divided by 27.4 in the year that you turn 70 1/2 Whatever the value of your account is on December 31, divide that sum by 27.4, and that's the amount you have to take out in the first year. You can delay the first year's withdrawal until the next year, but then you have to take out two payments.

It comes out to about 3.6%. That percentage goes up every year with every year you live. Not only that but if you fail to withdraw the money from each category, you receive a 50% penalty…and you still have to pay tax on the full amount! If you were supposed to take out $50,000 and you didn't do it, the government charges you a penalty of $25,000, and you still have to pay tax on the full $50,000!! Unless it is a Roth IRA. This is a case of having to understand the tax laws. The IRS is serious about getting their tax money, and it may pay you to have a professional financial consultant and tax specialist guiding you with your decisions.

A lady came into my office a couple of years ago. She had a teacher's retirement account, IRAs, and a few other things, and someone told her she could combine her retirement accounts and just withdraw from one if she wanted. That is simply not true. Luckily for her, she was still in the 60-day window, and we were able to unsnarl the mess. Otherwise, she would have been pushed into a higher tax bracket and unwittingly paid much more tax than necessary, as well as the 50% penalty on what she should have taken out but didn't. You can't combine IRAs with 401(k)s or 403bs for RMD purposes They are like zebras and giraffes…different animals and they don't blend. She had asked one question, and they had answered a different one.

She was very lucky. ***Smiling Retirees*** know that sometimes it's not what we don't know, it's what we think we know that simply isn't so, that gets us in trouble.

CHAPTER 2
QUESTIONS PEOPLE SHOULD BE ASKING...BUT ARE NOT!

We sometimes live in false confidence, believing we know what we need to know...and yet there are many times when something we needed to know wasn't even in our minds to ponder! The following section presents questions retirees should be asking, and are now offered here in case they have not yet been the focus of your thoughtful reflection in order to become a *Smiling Retiree*.

Question #1: How do I get enough net income to fund my lifestyle in retirement?

Every retiree or retiree-wannabe needs to ask this one. The key words in the question are "net income", which means income after taking into account income taxes and inflation. Selling off the mutual funds in your retirement account is NOT income.

Most people that I run into are investing almost exclusively for growth. This is great while you're young and trying to accumulate enough wealth to eventually live comfortably off the earnings from your assets. However, investing for growth can be chancy when you're approaching or in retirement.

Balance is the wisest approach.

Most young people, starting their investment journey at say age 25, don't have very much money. Their first priority is accumulating wealth. As you near retirement, somewhere around maybe age 55 or 60, it's time to start switching your investments from growth to the preservation of your hard-earned money.

The most important question is **"How do I get enough net income after taxes and inflation to fund my lifestyle in retirement?"**

You can receive income from rents, royalties, interest, and dividends. Everything else is just selling off your assets, which can quickly get you into serious trouble if you have enough assets that let you live off rents, royalties, interest, or dividends, great! You have arrived! If not, you have harder choices to make.

As I write this, stocks in the S&P 500 are paying an average of just under 2% in dividends. In most parts of the country, you can get around 4% or 5% from rental houses if they have no loans. Bonds are now near their lowest returns in your lifetime, with the 30-year Treasury bond in the 3% range. You can earn more with corporate bonds, but then you also have a higher risk. You and your professional advisor will have to evaluate how much risk you should take so you can have a decent income without undue risk.

Let's say you have $1 million… you can earn $20,000 to $40,000 per year, gross income if you don't have this money in a Roth IRA or life insurance cash value, you'll have to pay taxes on that income. Real estate and stocks will have some tax advantages, but the bonds will not. Also, bonds will be riskier because of the potential for default risk and interest rate risk. If rates go up, the bond value will go down. If you have a long time to go before the bond matures, it could go down a lot. Of course, you can just hold the bond until maturity and get your money back, plus the return, assuming whoever issued the bond has the money to pay you. The way to think about bonds is as a means to **lock in interest rates.** If you are satisfied with the interest rate and the quality of the issuer of the bond, you could choose to employ some bonds in your portfolio.

Having guaranteed income in your retirement will probably let you sleep peacefully. Fixed annuities will give you guaranteed income. You might want the variety that gives you guaranteed withdrawal benefits over your lifetime as opposed to the variety that you can only annuitize. If you annuitize an annuity, you lose all flexibility, which means you can't adjust your income or reach in and take out more money if you need it. If you go for the guaranteed income withdrawal though, most of the companies will let you stop the income if you wish. Also, if you die before you use up your pot of money, your heirs will receive the balance. Some companies will even let you get increasing income, so in some ways, this can be the best of all worlds. If you have fixed annuity accounts inside Roth IRAs, you can get true tax-free income along with increasing income.

Be sure you understand the different scenarios that exist with fixed annuities since there are many variations. With a fixed annuity the earnings are at risk, but the principal is guaranteed by the insurance company. With a variable annuity, both the earnings and the principal is at risk. That could be acceptable if you are comfortable with the risk and the fees, but as you get closer to retirement, you may need less exposure to risk. Be mindful of the penalties for early withdrawal.

You can also mix in some life insurance cash values. Should you overfund an insurance policy, you can take income out that is tax-advantaged.

You have to do all of the above correctly of course, but if you have good advice and construct a portfolio of several of these assets with an eye towards income rather than growth, Smiling Retirees can maximize their income in retirement while completely or partially protecting their hard-earned money.

> "A good decision is based on knowledge and not on numbers."
>
> Plato

Question #2: Who should I be dealing with?

This was answered rather thoroughly in FAQ #9, "How do I know if my advisor and I are compatible?", but just to be on the safe side, here is the short answer.

You want to work with a professional who specializes in what you need. As you get closer to retirement, you'll probably need a financial advisor who has experience preserving wealth, someone who can help you figure out the best ways of earning income as a retiree.

The market is a great place to accumulate wealth, but it may not be so great for preserving it. Having most of your money in the market when you're near or in retirement may subject you to more risk than you will find acceptable. It is fine if you have enough assets to comfortably live off of the dividends. But for most Americans approaching retirement as I write this, that is simply not the case. You're risking everything you've built.

Think about it this way: "What's the next 20% move in the market? Is it most likely to be up or down?"

It's great if the market falls down 20% if you're just starting out, because then you can probably buy shares at a lower price. But if you're close to or in retirement and withdrawing money, and you lose 20% or more, that can spell disaster.

So that's the point. Who should you be dealing with? You might have been dealing with a professional that helped you accumulate all that money, but that person may be the wrong advisor when you get older, and your financial needs shift.

When you get to 70 years old, you're probably seeing an internist or cardiologist or a rheumatologist, not a pediatrician. You may not be interested in buying a sports car anymore; now you're buying a safe, solid SUV. This doesn't mean that all of your money has to be in protected savings vehicles. But you need to be dealing with someone who has the same mindset that you have.

So that's who *Smiling Retirees* are dealing with …a financial specialist who provides what they need.

Question #3: What is a good investment strategy?

One of the best possible strategies is dollar-cost averaging. In other words, put your money into a few selected stocks month after month, quarter after quarter, year after year, decade after decade. As the price rises and falls, you'll be purchasing new shares at different prices, and over time your shares will have a lower average cost per share and thus accumulate money faster. This, of course, assumes that you have picked companies whose stocks actually go back up.

When you invest in something that fluctuates a lot, it will probably do pretty good. It always has, assuming that it eventually goes back up. The problem is that dollar-cost averaging in reverse also works, so when you start taking money out, it can go down faster. When you put money into an investment that fluctuates, or you take it out for that matter, you can end up with a lower average cost per share. When you're putting money in, your funds go up faster, but when you withdraw, the funds go down faster. Smiling Retirees know that dollar-cost averaging is a great way to accumulate money, but not so good to preserve it and receive income.

Of course, allocating your money over the five major areas of investments can also be a good investment strategy. You can put money into stocks, bonds, real estate, cash in its many forms, and commodities, like gold, silver, oil, and diamonds.

You could find great companies to invest in. Then, wait to invest until those companies are selling at bargain prices to buy. How do you know which are great companies? You can use some logical criteria such as high return on total capital. That particular measure can be an indication of good management because it looks at how management has handled the total capital that they have employed. Most people don't have the patience to do this, but it is a very good investment strategy if you can stand waiting for the right time. Remember, there are no called strikes in investing. You can just wait for the right pitch, as Warren Buffet has been fond of pointing out.

Well placed real estate is another very good investment strategy. If you have a rental house with little or no debt, you can probably get a decent income that should grow to keep up with inflation.

Preserving some of your money in saving vehicles like treasury bills, fixed annuities and CD's is yet another strategy that most retirees need to consider.

Pick the one that is paying the most at the time you are investing. And be sure to read the risk disclosures available in your state. You can always shift back into the markets after they have their next decline, assuming that there is one again.

There will be investment professionals available to help you in each of these areas if you don't have the time to do it yourself.

Smiling Retirees know that the best idea is to find a specialist who has experience in all of these areas.

Like every other question, it all depends on your income and preservation needs.

> "Those who have knowledge, don't predict. Those who predict, don't have knowledge."
>
> Lao Tzu

Question #4: Should I try to get most of my money into the tax-free category? If so, how?

Let me reiterate; taxation is probably the biggest expense of your entire life! The best way to understand taxation is by recognizing its three categories:

1. **Tax now**
2. **Tax later**
3. **Tax never**

We should probably call the "tax never" category the "tax-advantaged" category, but we really would like the proceeds to be tax-free if possible.

So what would be in there? Roth IRAs, ROTH 401(k)'s, ROTH 403(b)'s and life insurance cash values are the only investments that are truly tax-free. The chances are good that if you're presently working, you're contributing money to your company's 401(k). You could simply have the administration shift part of your current or future funds into a Roth 401(k) if they have that alternative. You will have to pay income tax now, but then all earnings and withdrawals will accumulate tax-free. One further quirk is that money still in a ROTH 403(b) or ROTH 401(k) at age 70 ½ requires that you begin required minimum distributions.

It's an unfortunate circumstance, but sooner or later you'll have to pay taxes on your tax-deferred retirement account withdrawals. The only choice is when. This is why you may want to consider shifting some of your money now while you can stay in the same tax bracket and while the tax rates are still relatively low. Of course, always get expert counsel from your investment and tax advisor first.

You may also want to consider building up capital in life insurance cash values, but as with every financial decision, you must do the calculations first to know which choice is best for you. These calculations can become detailed, and since we don't know what we don't know, you may want to consult with a qualified professional who can help you achieve the results you desire.

The objective of all these strategies is that when you take your money out of your accounts, it will be tax-free, AKA tax advantaged. This way, you will have a more complete idea of your true wealth, and you may have saved a lot of money if, as I suspect, tax rates go up. You may also save tax on your social security.

Whenever you invest, Smiling Retirees always look at how a strategy could hurt them. Shifting your retirement funds into tax-free investments will hurt you if tax rates go down.

Not too likely!

> "Risk comes from not knowing what you're doing."
>
> **Warren Buffett**

Question #5: How do I plan for someone to take care of me later in retirement if I need help?

That's a doozy of a question.

This is a decision that should have been made long ago by buying long term care insurance. Most people don't buy LTC policies because they felt like the rates were too high when they were young, or the need was too far in the future to be a concern.

If you haven't purchased a long term care policy to help you in your elder years, there are several things you can do now. You may be able to purchase an LTC policy now; the rates will be higher than when you were in your 30s, but they may be affordable given your current circumstances. And, if you're insurable, you could shift some of your life insurance to the version that provides some home health care and long term care benefits. You can also shift some of your annuities over to the versions that provide some home health care and long term care benefits. This depends on the states you live in. Some states have those provisions, and some don't.

The best choice, of course, is having so much money that it really doesn't matter…but that is easier said than done.

Failing that, something I recommend is that you consider moving out of your large and difficult-to-manage house into some sort of group living community. These types of facilities are probably going to mushroom as 10,000 people turn 65 years old every day right now.

I recommend you look for versions that have multiple levels of assistance. Some facilities have townhouses that attach to units like apartments or are like the old-style hotels. Some communities may offer assisted living or nursing facilities. This way, you'll be able to use the different services as you age and your needs change, and if you apply when they are being built, you might benefit from good deals or incentives.

I also have clients who didn't move when they should have, and now they're older, getting dementia, and the kids don't know what to do, so take care of this earlier rather than later.

Most people don't want to move out of their home. You may have to at some point. I have heard people say, "Well, my kids are going to care of me. I took care of my daughter, and she will take care of me." Then the family has to decide who's going to give up their career because elder care can be a full-time job. It can become an impossible task.

Part of the problem, of course, is that people don't want to accept that they are aging or losing their abilities and they choose to avoid the issue rather than confront it. Then they wind up getting trapped with the rapid changes in their circumstances. As the population ages, this will become a much bigger problem, even epidemic. Smiling Retirees make a conscious decision while they are able.

Check to see if your county has health services with professionals who can help out. If you're living in an area where there is a student nursing program, you may be able to acquire student services for less cost. It's good training for the nursing students, and your expenses can be less while either you or your elders receive decent care. I know people who have taken care of their parents for 15 years and never had a day off. That's an unhealthy situation for everyone.

> "Information is not knowledge."
>
> Albert Einstein

Question #6: How do I fund my health care if I need help?

Some people think a way to fund their health care costs is to move all their assets into a trust for their family, saving their assets from being consumed by their healthcare costs while preserving the family wealth for their children. However, many states have a "five-year look back." This means that if you go into a nursing home where you're asking the government to help pay for your services, the state will look back five years and ask questions about your finances, such as if you've given anything away in the last five years. States are now talking about increasing the period from five to seven years.

An irrevocable trust is certainly one solution for funding your health care needs. This way you may be able to rely on government support after your family wealth has been allocated to a family trust and becomes unavailable for your personal uses. This is one solution for a couple where one of them goes into a nursing home, and the other one ends up essentially broke and with many years to live. The community spouse (the one not in the nursing home) needs to be able to get income to live on.

There are endless versions of this strategy, and you need very competent legal advice before doing this. You need an attorney who is well versed in the current and probable future laws in this area. Of course, part of the problem is that people are living longer than ever before, and in many cases exceeding their funds, becoming unable to live decently in their elder years.

An irrevocable trust is a separate entity. It has its own tax ID number. You have to be careful because a trust has the worst taxation, so as with everything, it's a trade-off. It's merely another one of the 107 legal and financial strategies available to you, and which you and your financial and legal advisor can weave together. *Smiling Retirees* know it just depends on what they want…and knowing what they *need*.

Question #7: Should we live in our current home until retirement?

This is a question people should be asking. If you and your partner are both active and healthy, it is OK and normal to live in your home into retirement.

You should at least look at this issue and consider your physical abilities, then go take a look at what else is an option. Find out about the community group living facilities that are available. Go visit them, and see if you like them. Can you visualize yourself living with the people there? If you're 66 and you go to one of these retirement communities, and everybody's in their 90s, you're not going to fit in…but if you're 73 and most of the people are your age, it might be okay.

The advantages are that you give up a lot of work and responsibility. You don't have to shovel the sidewalks anymore; you don't have to fix the roof....you no longer have all the problems that come with owning a house. Of course, you give up a lot of the benefits, too, but *Smiling Retirees* know that at some point in time someone will probably have to help take care of them.

You might also consider moving out of your area. If you're in a cold climate, wouldn't it be nice to live in a less expensive neighborhood somewhere in the south where it's warm, or maybe moving closer to the kids and grandkids?

> "To know what you know and what you do not know, that is true knowledge."
>
> **Confucius**

Question #8: What happens to my retirement lifestyle if a black swan event occurs?

A black swan event is an event that is infrequent with a very large impact, such as a volcano erupting after many years of lying dormant, or the appearance of a new comet. The term comes from a saying from the Middle Ages, something like "that will happen when you see a black swan" just as people might say "when you see a pig fly." Pretty unlikely.

Nobody ever saw a black swan until explorers got to Australia. They were all white. This term refers to an event that you don't see very often. It has been re-popularized in the great book, *The Black Swan* by Nassim Nicholas Taleb.

If you think about it, how many times do you have to see a white swan to prove that all swans are white? The answer, of course, is not many times. When you see a white swan, or anything else for that matter, it does not prove they will always be white. What has that got to do with becoming a *Smiling Retiree*? Quite a bit actually.

You hear theories all the time that the market, or some fund is returning "X" percent. The theory is that because they returned that amount over that time span, it will be the same in the future. We know that is not necessarily true, but once we hear a return number, it sticks in our mind. The real question is how many times do we have to see any theory confirmed to prove it? The answer, of course, is that we can never prove any theory. No matter how many white swans we see, it does not prove that all swans are white…but it only takes seeing a black swan one time to disprove the theory. Does the market ever go down? Of course. But people tend to forget the negative events and go right back to looking at the statistics to manage their money.

Financial black swan events do occur periodically. Think of the dot-com crash of 2000, or the 2008 market crisis; these can be considered black swan events. While there can be positive black swan events, most often we are referring to the market going down. Though not frequent, it could have a very large impact…so you have to ask yourself how a black swan event will affect your account.

Galileo, you'll have to simplify the experiment.

If you're twenty-five years old or just starting out, it'll probably be a positively fantastic event because you'll be able to buy investments at lower prices. If you're 55 – 70, you're nearing or already in retirement, you're taking money out of your accounts to live on, and it will be a really bad event. Smiling Retirees know they have to look at the consequences of events happening, not just the probability. It's pretty unlikely that your house is going to burn down, so you will probably have more money if you don't buy fire insurance. Nobody does that, though, because of the consequences. It would be crazy.

Besides, it would be really irresponsible to not buy fire insurance on your house. Even though your investment portfolio is probably much bigger than your house, most people have no protection of any kind on their investments…and the probability of a negative event affecting your investment portfolio is much bigger than one affecting your house.

The *Smiling Retiree* considers the effect of a black swan event on his or her wealth and takes steps to protect their assets. Whether this is through true asset diversification, or purchasing put options on their stocks as insurance, or implementing other strategies for protecting their assets, the Smiling Retiree always prepares for the unknown. You don't have always to be worrying about this, just be prepared. Consult with your financial specialist to make sure a black swan event doesn't compromise your financial future.

Financial Success: For the Smiling Retiree

Question #9: What if I convert to a Roth IRA and the rules change, increasing the tax on my future withdrawals?

Though rules change all the time, tax theory says to tax either the seed or the harvest, but not both. The likelihood of the IRS or Congress making changes that change the original tax arrangement with the American public seems unlikely. This would be a true black swan event.

In my opinion, I don't think this will happen for two reasons. First, most retirement accounts are not in Roths, so Roths would not be a high-profile target for a tax change. Most of the money in retirement accounts is in tax-deferred accounts because people find it very difficult to write the check that converts their funds to a Roth. I believe most of America's retirement money will stay in taxable accounts, and this makes it much more likely for the government to fight and win the battle for increasing tax on tax-deferred accounts rather than the battle of double taxing Roth IRAs. As I write this, only about 3% of the money in retirement accounts is in Roths. The rest is in the ticking tax time-bomb accounts of IRAs, 401(k)s, 403(b)s, etc.

The second reason is that our culture usually accepts "grandfathering" as a way for separating current and future differentiation, honoring agreements made prior to new decisions affecting the future. So, if you do not have a Roth IRA now, set one up. If you are not working, you can still convert some of your qualified retirement money to a Roth. You could even convert $100. At least you have then entered the Roth system. If the government does away with the Roth in the future, you are still in the system.

You might wonder if you can be a patriotic American and use the tax fee Roth IRA system. Of course. I am not saying don't pay income taxes. I am only saying to strategically decide *when* to pay the taxes. Judge Learned Hand is famous for ruling that there is nothing sinister about so arranging your affairs that you pay the least amount of taxes that the law requires. I am only suggesting that you strategically figure out how to pay the least amount that is required over your lifetime. It may benefit you to pay some taxes now while you might be in the lowest tax bracket for the rest of your life. There are even very clever ways to combine all these strategies together to rescue your retirement accounts from the ticking tax time-bomb. The details will vary for each person. You need to get together with a specialist in this area if you have too much in the tax-deferred category.

Bottom line, the *Smiling Retiree* knows that if they can get most of their money into the tax-advantaged area, they will probably have more net income to fund their lifestyle in retirement.

Question #10: The company I'm investing in…is it risky?

A risky stock is one that is overpriced. You can have a lower risk company, but it may be a risky stock if it's overpriced. If you purchase an overpriced stock, you're taking the chance that the price may fall rather than the company growing into the price per share you paid. The truth is that ***any investment is worth the present value of the future income.*** With some companies, you can have a pretty good idea of their future income. Most you really can't.

Always ask yourself, "Is this company going to most likely still exist and dominate its market place 10 or 20 or 30 years from now?" Great consumer franchises probably will. Many rapidly rising tech companies…you have no idea. Their great new idea may get replaced by some new technology that hasn't even been invented yet. Suppose you were restricted to only a few investments in your lifetime. What if you could only pick, say, four companies to put your money into for the next three generations to take care of your family? If you are buying individual companies and you can live on the dividends, that may be a better way to choose.

There are other elements that could make a company risky such as a weak management team, or the flagship product is aging and losing its market share, or their capital investments in machinery is lagging and giving the competition an edge...

However, generally, the biggest risk factor is the company's debt. Excess debt is what usually kills all enterprises, so if you start with low debt companies, you may have a better chance of minimizing your investment risk. No matter how good the industry is, if the company is over-leveraged, there is more risk. The point is that a conservative company could have a risky stock if the stock is overpriced, and even great companies can get into trouble if they have too much debt.

So let's ask this question: "What would be a Warren Buffett kind of company?" He looks for companies with low debt which have some sort of consumer franchise. Buffet's example is if you're standing in line at the grocery store and you see a Hershey bar for sale for a dollar, you're probably not going to go across the street to buy an off-brand for $.75. Hershey's has a consumer franchise. Who else does? Coca-Cola, probably the most recognized brand in the world. Could they have some debt? Sure, particularly now when we have these extremely low-interest rates. The stock may still be risky if the ***price*** gets too high, even if the company is stable.

Right now, if you saw a bond that yielded 8%, you should wonder, "Why would that company be willing to pay 8%?"

Banks would probably charge it 4% so that it might stand out as a more risky company. The Smiling Retiree always asks questions that try to get to the truth.

Question #11: How do I know if my advisor and I are compatible?

This is probably the most important question you could ask about every professional you work with, in every area of your life. It is particularly important when you are doing retirement planning.

First of all, since you're looking for guidance with retirement investment planning, you should find a professional who specializes in this financial area, and you want someone with many years of experience advising pre-retirement and retired clients.

Interpersonally, there are some factors you should consider, such as:

- Do we get along?
- Are our values the same?
- Do we like speaking with each other?
- Are they fun to work with?
- Do they have the experience to guide me through this new area of my life? You might need a professional guide

rather than an old fashioned roadmap or a little brochure that you read over the weekend.

- You could look at various business temperaments. Is he or she business business, business relational, relational business, or relational relational?

- Are they fixed on just one strategy? If you go to a specific car dealer, chances are that the suggestion they give you will be their brand of car.

- Are they free to use any investment and strategy that fulfills your needs?

Most of the world right now is invested for growth, but there is a giant tidal wave of Americans hurtling toward retirement. As I write this, someone is turning 65 years of age about every 11.5 seconds! When you reach the magic age of 65, you are probably close to retiring, and if you own your own company, you probably think you have another five or 10 years, or more, and maybe you do. The point is when you do retire there are some significant financial changes to expect.

- Will you be adding new money into your Social Security and Medicare accounts? No.

- Will you still be adding new money into your IRA or your 401(k), or 403(b) at work? No.

- Will your employer add new money into both of these systems for you? No.

Actually, these benefits reverse and most Americans begin withdrawing funds from these systems. This occurs at the rate of about 10,000 people every day right now, including weekends. All the money that used to go into these systems is now coming out.

This is a big sea change for you financially, and also for the economy as a whole, and you'll need to alter strategies. The financial advisors and strategies that helped you *accumulate* money may not be the best professionals to help you *preserve* your money. My best advice is that you need to work with a specialist, just as in every other area of your professional and personal life. We frequently live our lives by shortcuts like sayings and adages. "If you always do what you always did, you will always get what you always got," is not the right adage to use when you are going into retirement.

When you seek medical advice at your age, there is no point going to the pediatrician you might have seen as a child, because pediatricians specialize in medical issues for younger people. You need doctors who are specialists in preventing and treating ailments for people of your own age, and it's the same thing with finances. However well-intentioned your financial advisor may be, they may not have the knowledge or experience to effectively guide you toward a successful retirement financially. You need to find a professional who specializes in generating income, and preserving and distributing your wealth if you are approaching or in retirement.

This will be a lifetime relationship, in the full sense of the word. The person you seek has to be likable. Does their investment philosophy match with yours? If you're a conservative investor, is their investment philosophy suitable for yours? Is this person willing to help you preserve and grow and distribute your money? Can they help you plan strategies to achieve this? Are they versed in minimizing the effects of taxes and rising costs on your hard-earned wealth?

The professional you select has to understand taxes and calculate the impact of various tax strategies on your lifestyle because taxes are probably going to be the biggest expense in your life, with the possible exception of medical expenses. Former Controller General David Walker thinks the government will have to double taxes shortly, certainly within the next seven years at the latest. It doesn't matter as much how much return you make because if you don't do tax planning properly, your gains can be entirely wiped out.

You want an experienced advisor, someone who's gone through many market cycles, and helped many people navigate the quicksands of retirement. A recently released study claimed that the average age of fund managers in the "dot com" crash of 2000 was 27, which means they were only 14 years old when the largest crash that ever happened occurred in October 1987. They were only nine years old when the great bull market of the '80s and '90s started. The point is that for most of their lives, the market had only been going up…until the three-year bear market in 2000-2002 when the NASDAQ lost over 80% of its value, and many dot-com companies disappeared. Clearly, you want a professional financial advisor with significant experience in market cycles and a steady, reasonable hand at the controls. Even then, there is no guarantee of success.

> "It is easier to stay out then get out."
>
> Mark Twain

Financial Success: For the Smiling Retiree

CHAPTER 3
INACCURATE BELIEFS PEOPLE HAVE ABOUT INVESTING

Over the years, there are wealth-related "truths" we've heard, or read, or been taught by our family and friends. We have accepted them because of the source...credible, logical, relevant, persuasive...and yet these accepted "truths" may actually be the antithesis of fact and professional practice.

Gathered here are ten common myths Smiling Retirees should recognize as harmful to the security and income production ability of their retirement portfolio.

Myth #1: The market has returned 6% so I'll be okay if I take out 4%.

That would be true if somebody drops 6% into your account every year. If that happens, your account will grow. But how likely are you to earn 6% a year, every year, by investing in the stock market? By the market, we mean the overall market, like the S&P 500 for instance, an index of 500 stocks representing about 80% of the market value of all public companies in the USA.

It might be the market's average return over some specific period, but what does that have to do with how much you will earn each year in retirement?

Even more important than the average return is the sequence of returns. If you looked at the last 35 years, markets have been pretty fantastic overall. As I write this, if you started with a big pile of money 35 years ago and invested it in the S&P 500 Index, it would be worth over ten times that today. Of course, you can't invest in the index, although you could have invested in each of the stocks in the index, or invested in a mutual fund closely shadowing the index.

However, most people in America didn't start out with a big pile of money. Most people have put money into their retirement accounts, primarily mutual funds, a little bit at a time…month after month, quarter after quarter, year after year, decade after decade. If they are lucky, their employers have matched the money they contributed every month. If they are really lucky, their employer contributed all of the monthly investment.

That 6% return is meaningless because it only applies to the money that was in the account from the beginning. However, just for the fun of it, let's consider the following.

What would happen if all of the negative years came at the beginning of the 35-year analysis? If you had all the negative years in the beginning and did not add or subtract any funds, would you have more or less money at the end of the 35 years?

Suppose, instead, all the positive years were in the beginning and the negative years came at the end? Now, what do you think would happen? Would you have more money or less money at the end of the 35 years?

Here is the answer, and it is surprising. If you didn't add or subtract any funds from your original investment, you'd have precisely the same amount of money whether the negative years came at the beginning or at the end. The Commutative Rule of Multiplication means that it doesn't matter where you put the negative performance years, as long as you're not adding or subtracting anything to the original amount.

The real question is "What happens when you start taking money out to fund your lifestyle in retirement?" Here is the kicker! The vast majority of Americans are going to be withdrawing money from their retirement accounts in retirement, and *when* these negative years occur, matters vitally. Even if you don't want to withdraw any money out of your qualified retirement accounts, you have to start when you are 70½.

Let's say you start withdrawing money to live on in retirement and all of the negative years are at the end. Even if you grow the amount that you withdraw by some inflation rate, to keep your purchasing power the same, under most scenarios, you will have more money left after 35 years than when you started.

But what happens if the negative years are all at the beginning? Under most periods you would have run out of money in 10 to 15 years. This is pretty amazing since the ***average return*** is the same in the two scenarios. In one case you prosper, and in the other you are broke. And the only difference is when the negative years occur. This is an exaggeration to prove the point, to be sure. Neither case is going to happen in real life. But it is true that you can be severely damaged if negative years start happening after you start withdrawing money.

The determining factor for this was where the negative years were located. The placement of the negative years matters when you're withdrawing.

It's also vital when you're adding money to your account. Let's say you put in some money and the market drops in half when you're 25 years old.

My daughter called me up in 2008 and said, "Oh, my gosh, Dad, what am I going to do? My 401(k) dropped in half!" What do you think I told her? "See if you can double your contribution, because you are buying right now at half price, and you have a long way to go before you need it."

If you could get the market to drop 50% the first month, you start putting money in, hallelujah! That's because you'll be buying at a lower price and you'll be purchasing bargains. You are dollar-cost averaging, so you'll end up with a lower average cost per share, and your account will probably go up faster. This assumes you are picking good stocks or funds, and have some significant time left before you need the money. Investing a fixed amount into anything that fluctuates periodically in price will end up in the end with more money, assuming that it actually goes back up. Of course, this doesn't work if you have picked extreme investments like the dot-com companies of the late 90s and they go out of business. When you retire and begin withdrawing, though, the exact opposite occurs. Dollar-cost averaging works in reverse to give you a lower average cost per share just as it did when you were accumulating. The problem is that it may make your account go down faster, not up faster when you are withdrawing.

For years you've heard the experts talk about withdrawing 4% a year from your retirement account, alleging that you'd be all right, that you probably wouldn't run out of money. Well, a recent study concluded that the withdrawal percentage for you to not run out of money is actually 1.8%. If that's so, you then have to ask yourself, "Is it really worth the trouble to go through all of this risk just to take out 1.8% per year?"

If all your retirement money is in the market, that's not a great preservation strategy. On the other hand, let's say you leave half your money in the market and put the other half in different saving categories that provide you with income. This way, you don't have to touch the money that's in the market, and you're generating income from guaranteed sources to fund your lifestyle in retirement.

Most people think if you have 30 years to invest, you just keep socking your money away, you'll have up years and down years, but you'll be fine as long as you don't pull money out before it's time. But imagine you get to the month before you retire, and the market drops in half. Not good. Someplace during those years, the Smiling Retiree switches to a strategy that begins to preserve the money.

Myth #2: The Stock Market (Mutual Funds) Is the Only Place for My Money.

I don't know if anyone really believes the stock market is the only place to put their money, but it is the easiest. You can easily invest in stocks and bonds through a 401(k) or your own online brokerage account. If your company's 401(k) has a bond fund, you could put some money in it…but this may be the worst time to buy bonds ever, in our lifetime. This is because interest rates are near a lifetime low, as I write this...and if interest rates go up, bonds in your investment portfolio will go down.

I've mentioned the five investment categories before (stocks, bonds, real estate, various forms of cash, and commodities...gold, silver, palladium, platinum, diamonds, things like that...) It actually wouldn't be a bad idea to have some money allocated to each of these categories (with the possible exception of bonds right now). Great wealth has been accumulated in all five of them.

Investing in cash vehicles can also provide a slow but steady return if they're in a safe investment. Let's call them what they mostly are...savings vehicles. Some can get kind of fancy. You have a choice of Treasury bills, fixed annuities, bank savings accounts, CDs, and fixed life insurance cash value. I know, Treasury bills are technically securities, but I think most people are pretty comfortable with the idea that the US government will pay back the money in 30 days. Some of these products can be linked to market indices, so you have a chance of making more money than just the fixed rate kind. You can even have FDIC insured market-linked CD's.

Each of the five basic categories has many choices. You can buy a local rental house, buy a real estate investment trust, or buy apartments. You may not want to buy stocks that are related to real estate because these may be more correlated to the market and subject to market fluctuations based more on what is going on in the stock market than the real estate market.

Real estate's a great accumulation vehicle if you use debt to leverage your position, but leverage also causes risk. As you get close to retirement, why not adjust your thinking and use real estate as a source of income? With real estate, you surrender liquidity, but you will have rental income and maybe even property appreciation. My warning is not to count on any appreciation in any of your investments; let that be a surprise bonus. Smiling Retirees only buy real estate because of its ability to provide income.

A bond, a stock, anything, I don't care what it is; you should only buy it based on its ability to provide income. Appreciation is too ambiguous to be counted on; you don't know if you're going to have any. When you count on the appreciation and not the income, you may be disappointed, and you might get into trouble. It's just not dependable. You might get appreciation, you probably will, but it is not a guarantee and what *Smiling Retirees* need in retirement is income.

> "Your net worth to the world is usually determined by what remains after your bad habits are subtracted from your good ones."
>
> Benjamin Franklin

Myth #3: If I Shift Money Out of My Retirement Account, I Will Pay Taxes.

If you take it out of the *retirement account system,* like the 401(k) system or the IRA system and receive a check, you will pay taxes unless you employ some sophisticated strategies to avoid it.

However, you can shift it around among those various tax-deferred accounts and not be taxed. You can even shift from life insurance cash value policies to other life insurance cash value policies, or annuities to other annuities and not pay taxes. You can even shift from life insurance cash value to annuities and not pay taxes because there are tax-free sections of the tax code, like section 1035, which allow you to make those shifts.

Why would you want to make a shift? Well, there's that little detail of required distribution at age 70½. Each category requires you to annually withdraw the legal sum, and together, this cash inflow could put you in a higher tax bracket. Your 401(k) is a category, your 403(b) is a category, your IRAs are a category, and your SEP plans are a category. The fewer categories you have, the less number of withdrawals you will have to make. If all your retirement funds are in IRAs, for example, you only have to make one withdrawal, and you have better control over the annually required distributions. You will still have to take out the same amount of money in total, but you can take it all from one IRA if you want. If you make a mistake and take withdrawals only from your IRAs and not from your 401(k)s at 70½, big problem. There is a 50% penalty on what you should have taken out and didn't.

Another possible idea, if you have a 401(k), is to take a non-hardship, in-service withdrawal from your 401(k) while you are still working and shift the amount into an IRA. Why would you do that? Well, you can do it tax-free, for one thing, if you transfer the funds from one custodian to the other. Another reason is that you want more choices than those offered through the 401(k). You can probably have the same investments in your IRA as you had in the 401(k) if you want. It will also allow you to stretch out the tax for your and your spouses lifetime, as well as your heirs, it you set it up correctly.

Is it possible you might want to shift your funds between your retirement accounts because a different account is providing a higher rate of return? Or less risk? Or more risk if you want, for that matter? Sure. If you might pick up potential extra earnings, why let your money sit where it is? In a 401(k) you're going to have a limited set of choices. If you shift the funds to your own self-directed IRA, you'll have a larger universe of investment choices.

By staying inside the retirement account system boundaries, the *Smiling Retiree* can shift money within accounts and control the number of required withdrawals while enjoying more choices at the same time.

> **"You may delay, but time will not."**
>
> **Benjamin Franklin**

Myth #4: I should defer income taxes on my retirement monies as long as possible.

All your life it has made sense, and paid, to defer your income taxes until sometime in the future because the tax rate has been going down…until about two years ago.

In the last two years of the Second World War, the top tax rate was 94%; it went down to 70% in the '70s, and five years ago it got as low as 35%. Now it's starting to go back up. As I write this, the top rate is 37%. You can add the investment surcharge of 3.8% to that. And certain phaseouts put the actual top rate even higher.

Top Tax Brackets

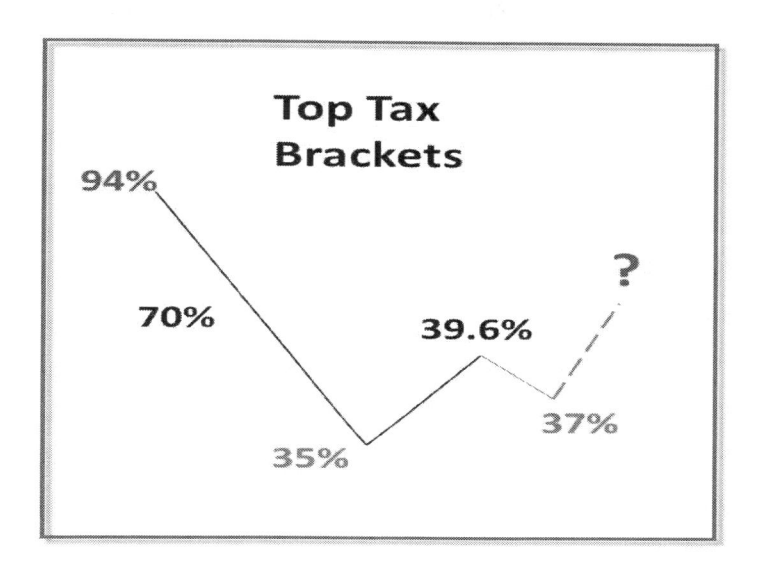

- 94%
- 70%
- 35%
- 39.6%
- 37%
- ?

You may want to subject some of your money to taxes now if you believe David Walker, the former US Controller General, who told Congress that they needed to double income taxes.

Here is a guy who probably knows more about the inner workings of the finances of the federal government than any human being on the planet. He ran the US Government Accountability Office (GAO) for ten years and in 2008, the year he resigned, the first group of Baby Boomers hadn't even started retiring yet.

By 2015, the Baby Boomers were retiring at the rate of 10,000 a day. Mr. Walker knew that when a person retires, they stop putting new money into their Social Security and Medicare accounts, and they usually start taking it out. Their employers also stop putting in new money into Social Security and Medicare for them. Projecting forward, Mr. Walker said that Social Security and Medicare were going to face serious hardships and recommended Congress double the taxes.

Already, tax rates are starting to go back up. The Big Question is, "How high are they going to go?" We were always told we'd have lower tax rates when we retired, but that may not be the case any longer if it ever was.

Most typical new retirees are surprised that they lose all their deductions…because they can usually no longer itemize. They may not necessarily go into a lower tax bracket and depending on how they arrange their affairs; they may even cause taxation on their Social Security income. They may not want to take money out of their 401(k)s and their IRAs, and they might avoid doing this for a few years, but it's mandatory when they reach 70½, which is only a few years down the road after they retire.

So this raises the question, *"How big you should let your tax-deferred accounts get?"* I've asked people, and the answer is always "As big as possible!" Well, yes, we want the most money we can have, but there's a ticking tax time bomb here.

What would happen if instead of putting your money into your 401(k), you put it into a Roth 401(k)? Yes, you'd lose the deduction, that's true, but think of this. While it has always been a genius move to deduct taxes when you're in a higher tax bracket and then withdraw your money and pay the tax when you're in a lower tax bracket, that's now likely reversed. It's likely that tax rates are going to go up. They have already started by going from the top bracket of 35% to 37%.

The question you have to ask yourself, and really should have been asking yourself all these years, is, **"How much money in that pot is really mine?"**

Let's say you have a house worth $500,000. You have a $150,000 mortgage on it, so you own $350,000 or 70% of your house. You would put $350,000 on your financial statement as your equity in the house. The lender is your partner. Every year that goes by, you probably pay down the loan, so the lender's portion gets smaller. And the house probably grows in value, so the lender's percentage gets even smaller.

Let's say you have $500,000 in your 401(k). Whether you like it or not, you have a partner in there as well…the US government. What's your partner's share of your 401(k)? The amount that you owe on future taxes will grow as your account gets bigger. It might also grow if the government raises tax rates.

For now, you can only tell how much of that money is yours if you can predict the tax brackets you'll be in during the 20+ years when you take out your share of the money. If David Walker's right, those tax brackets will be higher…your tax will be higher…your share will be less.

Now think of this! Your partner can change the partnership agreement every year. The rules can keep changing, and you can keep getting the continually shortening end of the stick.

The bottom line is that you really don't know how much of your retirement account is yours, do you? We pretend it's all our money, but it really isn't because you can't get it out without paying tax on it.

Deferring income taxes as long as possible is probably now a myth. It's been true all your life until the rates started going back up.

Here's another once-crazy but now-practical thought: Should you take your Social Security early…or should you use part of your retirement account instead? When it comes to paying taxes, which is the smarter choice? Only a calculation can tell.

You don't have a choice of paying or not paying your tax. Your only choice is when. You're in control of when you pay the tax, but that's it. You're not even in control of how much tax you'll be paying.

Something you can do to increase your control of the taxes you'll be paying is to look at the possibility of subjecting enough of your present-day deferred taxes to taxation while staying in the same tax bracket you're in now. This way you can, in a sense, prepay your future taxes at a lower rate, free assets locked in tax-deferred accounts, convert the cash into Roth IRAs, grow this wealth *tax-free* without the government as your partner, and stay in the same tax bracket you're in now.

The 10%-12% tax brackets… You will probably never see these again. It is for taxable income (line 10 of your tax return), for a couple up to $78,950 in 2019. If you get into the next tax bracket, it is 22%. Just above that is the 24% bracket. A couple can have taxable income in the 24% bracket up to $321,450. The numbers for a single person are $39,475 and $160,725. These numbers will almost certainly change for the worse in the future. In fact we know that they will revert back to the higher previous numbers on January 1, 2026.

Smiling Retirees start developing strategies that help them face this inevitability. Then they can select their best choice for their unique circumstances.

Let's say you have all your wealth shifted over to tax-free or tax-advantaged categories. Then, when you take withdrawals, you don't pay income tax. It doesn't affect the tax on your Social Security, and not only that but if taxes double, $2 \times 0 = $ what?

My calculation is zero.

On the other hand, if you're in a 12% tax bracket and tax rates double, now you're talking about some serious money. Remember that tax rates right now are historically pretty low

It's a Smiling Retiree who develops strategies that take into account what could happen that might hurt.

Having said all that, if you are already in the top tax bracket, you might need more current tax

deductions. It's a trade-off to be sure. Managing how and when to pay the tax can be a complex series of decisions involving not only how to best shift your funds between the categories, but which of the many available retirement plans that you can use. If you have your own business, you have the most flexibility, and, depending on your situation, there are ways that you can set up retirement plans to shift hundreds of thousands of dollars from current taxation at the highest brackets to later when you can deal with it and spread out the tax over time. This all depends on your specific circumstances and requires a series of careful planning sessions to come up with the plan that is right for you. Just know that there is almost always a way to greatly increase your families wealth in a tax-advantaged manner.

Myth #5: My income needs will be lower in retirement, so I can live on 75% of what I'm living on now.

Don't kid yourself. Most people cannot reduce their expenditures in retirement. You might be able to save a few bucks at the movie theater with your senior's card, or maybe eat for less at the senior dinner hour at your favorite restaurant…but don't expect you'll be able to cut back significantly. Let's say your expenses today are $8,000 a month. What can you cut from these expenses that equal a monthly decrease of $2,000? And if taxes go up, which I think they will, you'll have to cut back another…I don't know…another $500 a month? Go ahead, try it. Look at your monthly expenditures and trim them by 25%. I'll be surprised if you're NOT surprised by the difficulty.

Also, think of this. If you are still working, are you putting off anything you might like to do after you retire? If so, how are you going to do it if you cut back to spending only 75% of what you are spending now? Not only won't you get to do the things you were putting off, but you might have to give up a quarter of the things you are now doing!

You might really need more income in retirement than you are spending now. It all depends on your vision of retirement. Do you want to travel more? See the kids and grand-kids more? Fix up the house? Get new cars more often? Get a second house in a better climate for the winter? It's your vision, and you need to carefully think it through.

This is why I advise Smiling Retirees to plan on maintaining the same or an even better lifestyle in retirement than they have now, if possible. If anything, you may find your expenses increasing as you start doing activities you finally have time to enjoy.

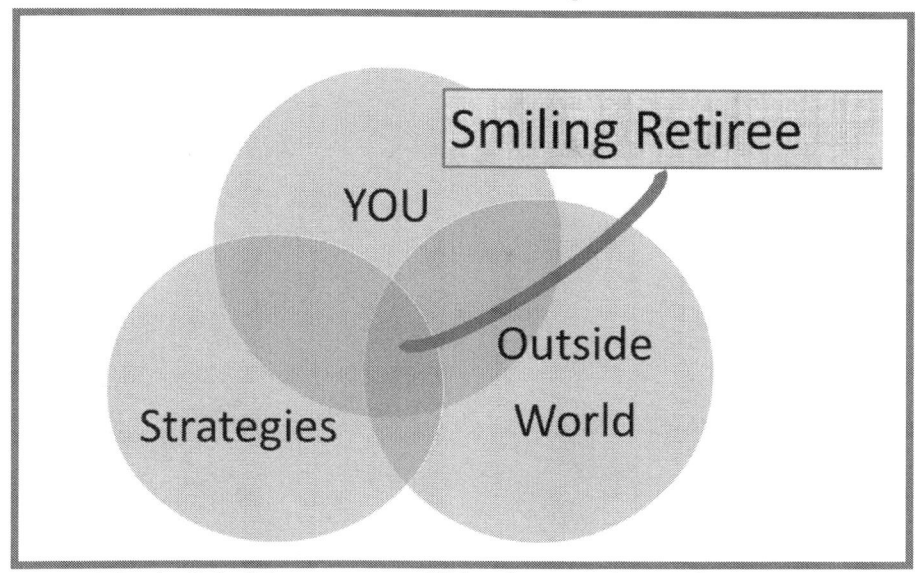

Myth #6: My taxes will be lower in retirement.

We talked about this in Myth #4, above. Taxes are probably going to start rising, so getting your wealth into tax-free, not tax-deferred accounts could be a smart strategy.

You also have to remember that your income probably will be lower, too. Also, you will probably not have the benefit of itemized deductions to keep your tax bill low.

When it comes to deductions, what do you lose when you retire? You lose almost everything. You're not deducting your kids anymore. They may be living with you, but you're not getting deductions for them. You are not getting the child tax credit. That is a double loss because the credit is an actual offset against your taxes. Hopefully you have your house paid off, so you don't have interest on it, and even if you're still making house payments, you're probably near the end of the loan, so the deductible interest amounts are lower. You lose your contributions to your retirement accounts, and you lose your contributions to your IRAs after 70½.

The only thing you do get is some extra standard deduction when you turn 65. You may get some medical deductions, although that has to exceed 10% of your adjusted gross income. You may have some charitable contributions, but frequently people in retirement are doing charitable work as volunteers, not making cash donations. There are, of course, strategies you can use that get you *more income* while also getting a current charitable deduction, but you have to carefully plan for them.

If you're eligible for Medicare, you'll have to buy supplemental medical insurance which could be a costly annual expense. Your pharmaceuticals might also be an expensive additional cost. None of these new and additional expenses are likely to be deductible unless they exceed 10% of your adjusted gross income.

You are now limited to a $10,000 deduction for all state and local taxes.

Your taxes will probably not be lower in retirement, your deductions will diminish, and your expenses will probably stay the same or increase. The *Smiling Retiree* makes plans that attempt to preserve wealth from taxation, and also create additional income.

Myth #7: Corporate earnings tell the story of the health of a company.

You can't rely on corporate earnings to tell the whole story, and here's why. When you and I make money, we can tell because we get a check. That's what we consider earnings. It's not the same with public corporations. Corporations have to file their earnings and taxes based on accrual accounting. It's a whole different process. You can look at a company's cash increase or decrease, and that will tell you some of the story, but then you have to figure out where that cash came from. Because corporations must use accrual accounting, they report income when the sale is made, and expenses are posted when the bargain is made to incur that expense. It's very different than you and I getting a check.

On the face of it, it's difficult to make investment decisions based on corporate earnings alone. Also, many American companies have huge earnings overseas, and those have to be "translated" from various currencies. Some companies with headquarters in other countries could have totally different accounting protocols. Sometimes when a company reports earnings or losses, what is really happening is changes in relative currency values. Is the yen, for instance, getting stronger or weaker than the dollar?

You also have to consider what the companies are reporting. The headlines might excitedly say, "ABC's earnings skyrocketed 100%!", But does that mean it went from $.01 to $.02, or does it mean it went from losing $5 and is now only losing $2.50? Were the sales being reported to a subsidiary? Were the to a customer, and then the company made a loan to the customer to pay for the sale? This was rampant in a frenzy leading to the dot-com bust in the year 2000. The company reported earnings increases, reported a current asset on their books called accounts receivable, and the executives received bonuses. The sales were not economic reality in some cases. These abuses have been curtailed by tighter regulations, but the point is that it is hard sometimes to get the full picture from the headlines. You have to be very wary when looking at company earnings. Headlines rarely tell the full story.

You have to have some understanding of accrual accounting if you're going to look at the earnings alone as an indication of the health of a company. Over time, a company's change in cash may help tell the story. Every public company now must report where the cash came from in their annual statement called the "Sources and Uses of Funds" statement. You can compare these changes over time to get some idea about what is going on within the company.

Smiling Retirees don't rely on corporate earnings' headlines as the full story of a company's health.

> "Where is all the knowledge we lost with information?"
>
> T. S. Eliot

Myth #8: Published percentage returns show the effect of an investment's ability to make money for me.

Published returns are NOT reliable as an indication of what will happen to your money.

One of the biggest myths about published percentage returns is that they indicate an investment's ability to increase your wealth. The truth is these are just numbers, not indicators of increasing or decreasing wealth. The concept is an illusion.

Think of this. Let's say over the last thirty years you designed two investments. One steadily went up from $10 a share to $30 a share. The other one started at $30 a share, went down to $10 a share, and then back and forth, up and down. You'd have more money in the one that fluctuated, yet the stated return would be 0% because you started at $30 and ended at $30. The reason you'd have more money is that you bought more shares (dollar-cost averaging) when its price went down.

You might wonder why the company reports them if these returns don't really indicate what you will make on an investment. The regulators noticed that in the past, companies cherry-picked the period over which they reported their returns. You would see an ad that told you how great one investment did from, say, the bottom of the market decline in 1987. Another company might pick a different period. You couldn't really compare how different investments had performed because they all used different periods. That's why the regulators made a rule that companies had to all use the same periods: year to date, one year, three years, five years, and ten years (or the life of the fund). At least now they are consistent. Be careful of the last number, though. The life of the fund could be from when it was started, which might be from the bottom of the last decline if it is less than 10 years.

My point is that the numbers people look at are mythical as to what is going to happen in the future. The **Smiling Retiree** understands the variety of influences that underlie the numbers, and that the numbers really don't mean anything important about the future. The reported returns only tell you what you would have if you started out with a big pile of money at the beginning of the period.

Myth #9: Bonds are safe investments.

Suppose you met me in October 1982 and I told you "I know a great investment for a piece of your money. This is an investment I think is fabulous; I think this could be the best investment chance of your lifetime". I tell you about it, and you go and talk to your barber and your brother-in-law (no offense to barbers and brothers-in-law) and all the other people you talk to about your investments and who give you financial advice. They say the investment I'm recommending has been going down since 1965. Don't do it!

What would you have missed by not following my advice? You would have missed 18.1% for the next 30 years on a 30-year US Treasury bond. That would probably have been one of the better investments of your life, other than your spouse.

On the other hand, suppose you met me now, and I said, "I think you should *not* pour money into that investment because for the last 30 years it has been going up in value and probably is near its peak. The only way it can go up much more is if interest rates go down more. And again, it is a 30-year Treasury bond, which is currently yielding 3%, as I write this. 18.1% down to 3% !! It got as low as 2.2% in 2017.

What would you guess you would have had to pay for a 30-year zero coupon Treasury bond in October 1982, which paid out

$1 Million at maturity?

$6,799.99 according to my financial calculator.

For under a $7,000 investment, you'd have $1,000,000 thirty years later!

That's pretty amazing.

How much do you think you'd have to pay right now? At 3% interest on the same 30 year, zero coupon bond would cost

$411,986.76.

Today, the best you could do is a little less than double your money on your investment over 30 years. In other words, this is the present value of $1,000,000 thirty years from now at 3 % interest

A bond is a tool whose purpose is to lock in an interest rate, and if you're satisfied with the current interest rate, buy the bond. If you're not satisfied, find a better investment for your assets.

Why else wouldn't you want to buy bonds? For one thing, you're paddling your boat upstream, against the current, because interest rates will probably go up eventually, right? They certainly can't go down a lot more! The next 5% move is probably going to be up, not down.

What about the risk of default? There could be a risk; just think about Harrisburg Pennsylvania when the municipality defaulted on its debt in 2014. Lehman Brothers, Bear Stearns… The bond index was called the Lehman Bond Index! Corporate and municipal bonds can default. What happens to bonds if interest rates go up? What happens if we have another recession? It's all a risk-reward trade-off. If you invest in a bond at these interest rates, will the reward outweigh the risk? What about a bond fund. There you will have no maturity date. Every year or so the fund manager has to sell off the existing bonds and replace them with bonds that are one year older in order to maintain the funds stated duration. If the rates are lower, the fund will now hold bonds with lower interest rates.

Of course, there are other reasons that people buy US Treasury bonds. Most people would agree that there is not much risk of default of the US government. If you have money in a foreign bank or a US bank way over the FDIC limit, say you are a corporate controller managing billions of dollars of your company's money, you might choose to put some into Treasury bonds. Just be aware of the interest rate risk. The shorter the time to maturity, the less the interest rate risk.

Like every investment, bonds carry a certain degree of risk and the Smiling Retiree understands the risk and diversifies sufficiently to weather any storm that may arise. Do you know the stock ticker symbol for the high-yield bond ETF?

JNK.

That's pretty symbolic and should certainly tell you something.

Every investment has a risk. Bonds are no exception.

Myth #10: The best place for my 401(k) is with my old employer.

Why do you want to leave your 401(k) with your old employer? Your soon-to-be, ex-employer's 401(k) plan? Sure, you could probably keep the funds in there forever…but do you think your employer's 401(k) administrators really want to be dealing with you and your heirs ~~out~~ into the far future?

Leaving your 401(k) with your old employer is rarely a good idea. Here's why. If you leave your money in your 401(k), can your heirs change custodians? Can your heirs add new beneficiaries? How flexible is it? In fact, can your heirs do anything except withdraw the money? It all depends on what the custodial agreement says. Have you read your companies custodial agreement? Few people have. But that is where all the rules governing your 401(K) are.

You also want to take into account that the custodians have protocols for managing your funds. Are the funds easily transferred when you want them? Are there mandatory waiting periods? The custodian may be difficult to work with…there are probably limits imposed through the 401(k) custodial agreement. On top of that, does your ex-employer's company have protocols that could inhibit the speedy transfer of your funds? Sometimes transfers can take months.

Remember, too, that 401(k)s usually offer only a select number of investments or portfolio choices, so you'll have to ask yourself if the available choices are right for you, now that you are seeking income and security, or could you acquire more appropriate investments outside the 401(k) program? Could you have the exact same investments in your rollover IRA if you wanted, while having more control and flexibility? Yes usually, assuming that they are standard publicly traded funds. On rare occasions, companies will have proprietary funds in the 401(k)s. That is pretty unusual nowadays.

Remember, as previously mentioned, there's the matter of being required to withdraw funds from every retirement category you own. When you are 70½ if you don't withdraw from each category, you could have as much as a 50% tax penalty.

Smiling Retirees have better ideas for their assets. Staying with the ex-employer's 401(k) program isn't necessarily one of them.

> "Perfection is not attainable.
> But if we chase perfection,
> we can catch excellence."
>
> Vince Lombardi

CHAPTER 4
TECHNIQUES PEOPLE COULD BE USING BUT ARE NOT.

It takes knowledge and experience to be aware of the many different possibilities for building, using and preserving wealth. Here are a few techniques available for those investors willing to plan ahead and educate themselves about new options for extra income, avoiding unnecessary taxation, and increasing their financial security.

Technique #1: Shifting funds to tax-advantaged investments.

Why shift your funds to tax-advantaged accounts? Because taxes are probably the biggest expense in your entire life. The more you limit your tax costs, the more money you'll have for yourself and your family!

The question now becomes, "How can I shift my investments to tax-advantaged accounts?"

First of all, all the funds in your qualified retirement accounts can be shifted to the tax-free category by converting them to a Roth IRA. "Qualified" means the account is officially categorized by the US government as tax-advantaged (tax-free or tax-deferred), such as official retirement accounts like IRAs, 401(k)s, and 403(b)s.

You can also shift non-qualified cash or fully taxable accounts to tax-advantaged accounts if you put them into specially designed life insurance cash value policies. There is a lot of criteria you need to look at before doing this.

As for the Roth conversion, there are arguments for and against doing this. Here's the argument against the conversion. Let's say you have $100,000 and it grows to $200,000; then you sell the fund and pay about 25% to taxes. That leaves you with $150,000.

If you have $100,000 and you pay 25% of it in taxes now, and then over some time it doubles, you still have exactly the same $150,000…so why would you bother converting to a Roth?

Argument Against Converting To A ROTH IRA

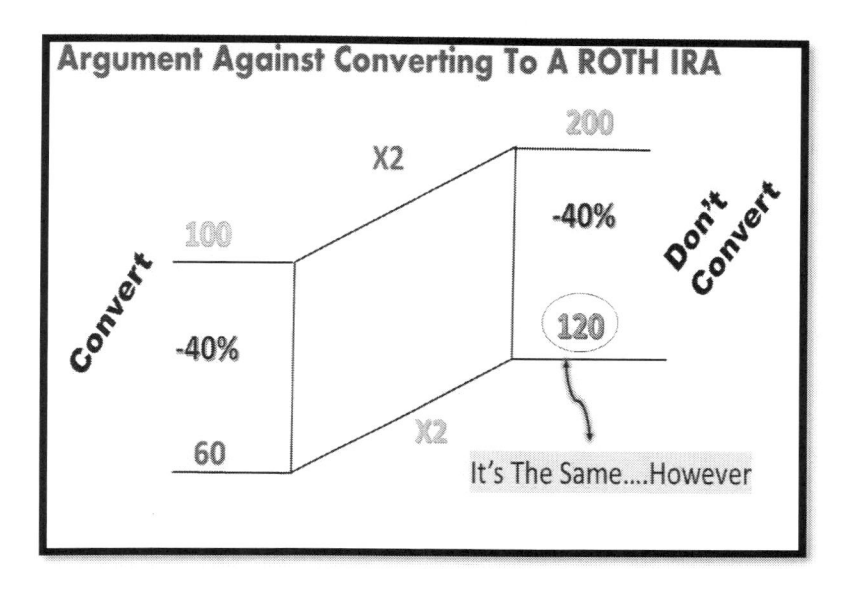

```
          X2         200
   100 ────────────────
    │              -40%        Don't
C   │                          Convert
o   │               ┌───┐
n   │               │120│
v   -40%            └───┘
e   │                 ↓
r   │         X2   It's The Same....However
t   60 ──────────
```

The amount you receive will be the same whether you pay the tax now or you pay the tax later, except for the following.

1. You might be in a higher tax bracket because you are earning more money or lose deductions when you take the money out.

2. The money you take out in the future may affect the tax on your Social Security benefits.

3. If you die and your heirs receive the money, they are going to have to pay the tax…probably at a higher tax rate than you would have.

4. Delaying conversion to a Roth could significantly hurt you if, as David Walker predicts, the tax rates themselves go

up.

The choice is not whether you pay the tax or not; the choice is only when you pay the tax…and when you do, you want to pay as little as possible. You might want to pay the tax if you can stay in the same tax bracket, but what if you don't? And, the current tax rates might be the lowest tax rates for the foreseeable future…maybe in our lifetime.

Shifting makes sense if these scenarios sound logical to you.

You can also shift your assets from investments that are taxed to the maximum as ordinary income, like interest from savings accounts, and bonds, to capital gains investments like real estate and stock.-And, you can also shift assets to trusts with charitable provisions and get a tax deduction! Nothing wrong with that!

Smiling Retirees consult with a specialist in this financial area.

Technique #2: Creating income from your stocks.

Let's say, that for whatever reason, you have a highly appreciated stock with no dividends. If you sell it, you know you'll have a lot of tax to pay.

What can you do? You have all this wealth trapped inside your stock, and you don't want to sell it because you'll get hit by taxes…yet you want to make better use of this wealth.

There are a couple of clever things you could do:

1. You can shift the stock into a trust that will benefit a charity at some point in the future. Once the trust is established, you can sell the stock within the trust, not pay a dime in tax, and then you can reinvest the proceeds to provide you with income for life. This income will be taxable to the extent <u>that it has had gains or earns interest</u> but may be offset by a charitable deduction that you got when you funded the trust. Eventually, the charity gets what is left, but in the meantime, you've increased your income. Also, if you don't want to damage your family's inheritance, but you still want more income, you may be able to take some of the new income you'll be receiving and ensure that the value goes to your beneficiaries tax-free. You can't do this exactly this way with stocks that are in a retirement account. There are some other much more complicated steps you can take if you have too much money in your retirement accounts and are afraid of the coming tax time bomb. They are different for each person and depend on your exact circumstances.

2. Here is a second technique. You can use this technique for stocks that are either in or outside of your retirement accounts. You can sell call options against the value of the stock. Let's say you have a stock worth $150.00 per share. You might be able to sell the 160 call option a few months out in the future. In other words, you give someone the right to buy your stock

anytime between now and the expiration date of the call option, the right to buy the stock from you at the strike price of the call. After fees, you might receive $4 per share. If you have 100 shares of that stock, worth $150,000, and you're not earning any dividends on it, you might get $4,000 every few months by selling calls. Do that four times a year, and you could receive $16,000 … over 10% … on an investment that otherwise is just paper wealth and a tax target.

Could the stock call get called away from you? Yes. However, as long as there is a time value in the call, you probably won't get called out. If the strike price of the call is above the price of the stock, any value is a time value, and the owner of the call probably will not throw that time value away and give it to you by exercising the call against you.

An exception is when a dividend is coming. If you are going to use this technique, you have to pay attention to when dividends are going to be declared. Start slowly and test the waters; do this on a very small basis at first, if you are going to do this at all. Keep doing this very small even after it has worked a few times. In fact, keep this trade very small until you have experienced it thru at least one big market downturn. As you approach the expiration date, which is the third Friday of the contract month, you can buy your call back and then sell a future one, covering your position. In a very real sense, you are renting out your stock and people are paying you for it.

You're going to want to offer a call far enough out in time, so you have time value, and you really have to know what you're doing.

This will take some homework, and perhaps the services of a financial advisor experienced in selling options on stocks, and you'd have to be open to a little risk because the stock could go down. But we are assuming that you already had that risk because you owned the stock to start with. This is a limited risk, but a person has to know what they're doing. You can't just say, "Wow! What a great idea!" and do this tomorrow. You'll have to get into this and practice it and become comfortable with this idea and its mechanics.

Of course, prior to buying or selling an option, investors must read a copy of the Characteristics & Risks of Standardized Options, also known as the options disclosure document (ODD). It explains the characteristics and risks of exchange-traded options. You have to know the characteristics of options, and at first, at least, you should probably work with a professional who really knows how to do this.

You also want to make sure there is volatility in the markets. If volatility is low, getting a high enough price for the options that you sell to make this worth the trouble could become a problem. Therefore, you'll have to know something about the Vix Index, which is also known as the Fear Index. Experienced traders say, "When the Vix is high, it's time to buy," meaning that the Vix is high when the markets are in chaos, usually after a big decline. You might want to buy stocks when the Vix is high because stocks have probably gone down a lot. On the other hand, "When the Vix is low, it's time to go" means that when no one has any fear, the markets may be overpriced and ready for a decline.

When you get really good at this, you might consider replacing the stock with an in-the-money call option. Your capital requirement will be much less as will your risk amount. You would have created what is called an option spread. There are endless varieties of option spreads. Here is a general rule of thumb. Buy intrinsic value and sell time value. That way the person on the other side of the trade will not make money unless the stock moves in their favor if you have this trade set up just right. And you will make money if the stock moves in your favor or just sits there without moving. This is not an area for the faint of heart. At least if you are putting much money at risk. The odds can be a lot better than going to the casino though if you learn the ins and outs of these strategies. Again, do all of this with a very small portion of your overall capital, if at all.

Smiling Retirees know they can use an asset that's not producing any income, and possibly earn 2% or 3% every quarter by renting the asset out as call options, possibly picking up 8% to 12% every year, which is a very compelling return in this market…or any market. Since your stock is simply sitting there and you're not making any money on it, you may be able to add to your monthly income by using your stocks in this manner, again and again, using appropriate caution and starting out very, very small. People get in trouble with this when they do it a few times and see it work, and then go out and load up on stocks. Then the market crashes and they lose money on the stocks.

This is another way to get income, and it could be right for some of your money.

> "We are drowning in information but starved for knowledge."
>
> John Naisbitt

Technique #3: Selling real estate (or highly appreciated stocks) without paying tax on the gain.

As mentioned in Technique #2, you can avoid the tax by deeding the real estate to a trust that will benefit a charity at some point in the future. Meanwhile, you could sell the real estate, turn the proceeds into income-generating investments and receive the benefit of the income that would otherwise be trapped in the real estate. You don't pay any tax on the sale of the real estate, and eventually, the charity gets some of the value while you get a current tax deduction on top of increasing your current income. Obviously that is the short version. There are many exact steps that you have to do correctly for this to work. However, there is a lot of money at stake, and you and your family may greatly benefit from using this technique.

Again, if you don't want to compromise your family's inheritance but want the extra income, employ some of the new income to ensure that your family members still inherit the full amount.

You could also start a family foundation. You must be careful about this because there are intricate rules to follow, but the family foundation could be another way of using your appreciated stocks or real estate in a manner consistent with tax law that may benefit your family as well as serve charitable purposes in the future. Wealthy families have done this forever, of course.

Of course, you could also do a hybrid and sell part of your assets and pay the taxes, while you let the other portion of your wealth provide income through the trust. It doesn't have to be all or nothing. You can choose to do a bit of both. You would have to do the calculations to decide which choice was better for you.

Always keep in mind your main purpose…what do you really need? An investment can only provide these five basic benefits:

- Growth
- Income
- Tax benefits
- Liquidity
- Some degree of safety or protection

That's all there is. You have to decide what you want, and what you need. Anything you select will diminish the extent of the others. It's like a blow-up balloon in a swimming pool. When you push one end down, the other end goes up. You can't get more juice out of an orange than is already inside, to mix our metaphors. There are only so many benefits from an investment. The art is in deciding what you are willing to give up to have what you really want and need.

Of course, we want it all, but a choice has to be made. We all want 15% interest, we want 8% income, we want all our money to be tax-free, we want 100% liquidity, and we want guaranteed safety…That is the best thing out there. But of course, it's not out there. It doesn't exist. You have to make trade-offs, as with everything else in our lives. You have to make a mindful selection.

Do you want to give up some liquidity for income? Or do you need to give up some growth for security? These are the types of discussions you have to have with yourself and your financial advisor until you can make a wise decision about how to satisfy your current, and more importantly, future economic needs. We don't have to completely give up any one category. We just have to decide what to emphasize most.

Since most *Smiling Retirees* need income, you're probably going to have to give up some liquidity, and maybe some growth, to experience the satisfaction of the benefits of more income.

> "I don't pretend we have all the answers. But the questions are certainly worth thinking about."
>
> Arthur C. Clarke

Technique #4: Creating family and tax-friendly entities to create more income.

Many people have wills requiring the personal representative to sell all the assets and then give some of the proceeds to selected charities. This will create a gigantic tax bill, of course, if the money is in their retirement accounts. Possibly a better idea is to move some of the assets, that are not in retirement accounts, into a trust with a charity eventually getting some of what is left, and benefit from the increased income now while getting a current tax deduction for leaving the same assets you are leaving anyway in the future. You just make the arrangements now.

For example, let's say you have a house and maybe your kids don't want it, but you like living there and want to live in it for the rest of your life. You can put the house in a trust with a provision that it goes to charity on your death. In the meantime, you can continue living in your home and everything stays exactly the same...except the government will give you a current tax deduction, you might lower your tax bracket, and you also eventually help your favorite charity.

I consult with people who have things they're going to leave to charity at their death, but they won't get a deduction for that. If, however, you arrange the details properly, you could get the deduction now, the charity will still get the property at your death, and meanwhile, you can increase your income. There are several different kinds of trusts that could provide outcomes like this, so it's best that you speak with your financial advisor or a tax specialist to identify the available choices so you can make the best decision for your circumstances. Ultimately an attorney has to advise you on the legal decisions you need to make regarding trusts. This planning must be done as a team approach between your financial, tax, and legal advisors.

You can also use this strategy with highly appreciated land, stocks, and business interests. The variations are endless. This is definitely not a do-it-yourself scenario. In fact, your advisors need to have a team approach to implement these strategies, as they will need to rely on a variety of specialists. These people will all cost some money. This won't be free because you will need calculations performed, documents drafted, and strategy sessions attended. However, the savings are sometimes tremendous.

Sometimes, millions of dollars.

You control the investments, sell the assets without generating current tax on the sale, get a tax deduction, and increase your income all at the same time, so why wouldn't you? *Smiling Retirees* know a good financial advisor can provide options such as this.

> "Don't gamble; take all your savings and buy some good stock and hold it till it goes up, then sell it. If it don't go up, don't buy it."
>
> Will Rogers

Technique #5: Sell at the top, buy at the bottom.

That's what everybody would like to do, right? It's the dream, but it rarely happens.

Something you could do is look at a graph and use a moving average to help you make buy/sell decisions. The moving averages people typically use are the 50-day moving average and the 200-day moving average. I don't much believe in technical analysis, but one of the tools people all across the world look at is the 200-day moving average of the S&P 500 stock index. When the S&P 500 drops below its 200-day moving average, a lot of alarm bells go off. People have that event programmed into their computer. In fact, they call that the Death Cross.

If you had simply bought the S&P 500 when it crossed above the 200-day moving average and sold it when it crossed below, you would have done magnificently well over the last 35 years. You would have mostly been in the market when it was going up and escaped most of the decline when the market was going down. You would not have hit the top or been out at the bottom. But you would probably have done massively better than the great bulk of people who got out at the bottom and couldn't stand it anymore and then poured their money back in when prices neared the peak

Here are some numbers that will raise your eyebrows: Before the year 2000, there had never been a $10 billion inflow into mutual funds in any one month. It got close in December 1999. Then in March, April, and May 2000, $50 billion went into mutual funds. To put this in perspective, in the October crash of 2008, on Black Friday, $50 billion went out in one day. Now that's what I call volatility!

So you can't ever really buy at the bottom and sell at the top consistently, but if you follow some common sense strategies, you can make a fair amount of money. What is it Warren Buffett says?

"All we try to do is be brave when other people are fearful and fearful when other people are brave."

I had three people come into my office a while back, and they told me they know how to manage risk and how to get out of the market when things start falling apart. Their perception is distorted because the market has been up for the last ten years, as I write this. People give more weight to what's happened recently. It's human nature and one of the behavioral finance laws that experts talk about. The most recent events are foremost in our minds.

I know they're not going to be able to get out because buyers begin to disappear when the market starts down. The bids disappear. The big institutional money managers are not going to be able to sell to each other. They can all see what's going on, and they all want out at the same time.

You should handle the risk mitigation by how much you allocate to each category, not hope that your money manager will get out of the market when the selling starts. The big institutions ARE the market. There is no one they can sell to! *Smiling Retirees* know millions of small investors are living with a dangerous illusion.

> Don't be the last guest at the ogre's dinner party!

> "Twenty years from now you will be more disappointed by the things you didn't do than by the ones you did do."
>
> Mark Twain

Technique #6: Diversify into different non-correlated

<u>assets.</u>

A great idea, of course, but almost nobody does it.

Most of America thinks they're diversified because they have different kinds of mutual funds. Even to the extremely limited extent that this could be diversification, if you look at those mutual funds, you'll see that a lot of times those funds have many of same stocks. What these investors are not diversifying is their *market risk* because when people start jumping out of stocks, they tend to jump out of everything

True diversification is when investments are absolutely negatively correlated, which means that as one asset class goes up, the other asset class goes down. There are only five asset classes:

- Stocks
- Bonds
- Real estate
- Cash in its many forms
- Commodities

Almost nobody is truly diversified. Some people tell me they're mostly in cash, waiting for the market to go down, but that's very rare. Most people are up to their necks in the stock market, and they're hoping their account managers will get them out.

Of course, the mutual funds can't get them out; the mutual funds ARE the market. Who can they sell to when and if there is another big selloff?

Take a look at most any big household name public company. The top dozen funds probably own 50% or 60% of these giant companies. Do you think anybody will notice if one of these funds starts to unload their favorite stock? Maybe the stock has reached the target price…or the manager is just locking in their profits before they disappear. Of course, the selling activity will be noticed, and when it is, bids for these stocks begin to slow and back off. When the whole market starts selling, the bids disappear. This doesn't happen very often, but when it does, you can't get out of your funds at the price you thought you could get.

So real estate, for instance, is completely non-correlated with stocks. If you have a rental house, it doesn't make any difference what the stock market is doing. It doesn't matter what interest rates are doing, or what bonds are doing. Commodities, which are such things as gold, silver, platinum, palladium, oil, and diamonds, are not correlated with stocks. They tend to move differently than the stock market.

It could be that the real problem is that nobody really talks about the five asset classes. It's easy to learn about these asset classes. For most people, it's just easier to put money in their 401(k) thinking everything will be fine.

Your financial resources are too important to waste or leave to chance, right? Speak with a financial specialist about really diversifying your investment portfolio to help protect your resources from sudden reversals. Smiling Retirees put their wealth into several asset classes and protect their wealth as much as possible from unseen storms.

> **The only difference between death and taxes is that death doesn't get worse every time Congress meets."**
>
> **Will Rogers**

Technique #7: Calculate the effect of various financial maneuvers.

If you had a business, would you bother to figure out the details of what would happen if you made an acquisition, or you financed a project, added a new product or decided to end a product line that wasn't working?

Of course, you would. So you just need to calculate what may happen if you make various financial maneuvers.

You are told just to go to those online calculators and input how old you are and how much money you want in retirement... Some of these online "tools" have an inflation rate calculator, but their key flaw is there is no way to look at the *sequence of returns.* They simply have you put in a guess as to how much the return will average. So it's not a truly useful exercise. In some years, you may have a 0% rate of return or even a negative rate of return. Even worse, none of those online calculators can help you figure out what's going to happen when you're withdrawing money, and the market starts going down.

You should regard your investments as a business. The calculators are not calculating the effect of different situations, and they should.

Remember, you heard it here first. There are three giant tidal waves coming:

- Rising taxes
- Rising interest rates
- Rising inflation

When do these hit? I don't know, and neither does anybody else. Although, remember former Controller General David Walker thinks they start to hit in 2020. At least he has said that he thinks taxes have to start going up by then. Since we can't predict the future, we need to take into account what happens to your money under various financial situations.

Smiling Retirees plan for the worst and hope for the best.

Technique #8: Seeing what the corporate insiders are doing.

If you're going to be invested in the markets, it might be a good idea to know what the company insiders, the people who run the company, are doing. Are they buying hand over fist or are they selling?

There are a lot of reasons why the directors, the CEO, or the CFO, might sell their stock. They might want to diversify, they might want to send their kids to college, and they might be buying a new house. If most of the company insiders are selling though, should we really be buying? They are in a better position to know the prospects of their companies than anyone else. If all of them are buying with their own cash, not just with the free stock options they receive, that's a pretty good sign. You can find this information online. If these executives are selling, you have to think, "Should I be buying from them?"

When you buy something, somebody is on the other side of that trade because the markets are a "net zero sum game" in the short term. Every buyer has a seller, and every seller has a buyer…if the sale goes through. ***Smiling Retirees*** think it's a good idea always to look and see what the corporate insiders are doing.

> "Beware of little expenses.
> A small leak will sink a great ship."
>
> Benjamin Franklin

Technique #9: Build a good financial team.

Nobody can know everything, and there is always a lot to know about what you don't know, or what you don't even know that you don't know…so it's a wise person who builds a financial team to help with the questions that always come up.

You need specialists with different areas of expertise like a financial advisor, a tax expert, a CPA, an attorney, maybe a real estate broker…professionals who can guide you through the ever-changing financial rapids. Your financial specialist will probably already have these other professionals available for you to work with as appropriate.

Consider that you might have outgrown the team you've been working with; as your financial needs change, there may be good cause to change the members on your team. I hear about this situation all the time. A farmer has an accountant who's helped him figure out the taxes on his farm, but the accountant has no idea how to help him plan for retirement…or how to minimize the taxes when he or she sells the farm and wants income from the value that's built up over the years. A good financial advisor will work with your current advisors as much as possible and appropriate to plan for your future.

You want somebody who specializes in what you need and has done it many times before. Most individuals are not going to have already an attorney or accountant, or financial advisor for that matter, who specializes in charitable entities that can save them enormous taxes on the sale of their highly appreciated land or stock or business interests, for instance.

Smiling Retirees know it's absolutely essential to have one professional coordinating all of this. Usually, it's your financial advisor. Otherwise, it's like taking different medicines from different doctors…the uncoordinated interactions can kill you.

CHAPTER 5
FUNDAMENTAL MISTAKES YOU MIGHT BE MAKING

Smiling Retirees know the value of challenging their core investment assumptions and practices. The strategies and tactics which once served a specific purpose may no longer be the best practice when the purpose changes, or when investment behaviors are inappropriate, creating flawed decisions resulting in flawed practices with limited or harmful results. Presented in this chapter are some fundamental mistakes investors may be making to their detriment and sorrowful ruin.

Mistake #1: Not switching from accumulation to preservation at the right time.

When you're 25 years old and have your first real job, your only financial goal is to accumulate wealth. One of the best ways to do this is with an investment strategy called dollar-cost averaging into the stock market, which was explained in Chapter 2. Another good strategy is buying real estate. Specifically a house you can live in, as you'll avoid paying rent and can instead build equity. Get a long-term fixed rate mortgage, fix up the house and property, and you'll be on your way to being a real estate baron. Both of these strategies…dollar-cost averaging and purchasing real estate…are great strategies for accumulating wealth when you're young.

Now fast forward 480 months (40 years), and you're suddenly 65 years old. Should you wait until the month just before you turn 65 to move your assets from accumulation to preservation? Probably not. It could be a disaster if the market reversed or had a big draw-down at this time. Your move from accumulation to preservation should have begun years earlier.

Think about this. Investment time is a miraculous asset because not only do you have years to save, and years to appreciate your wealth with market growth, but you also have the effect of compounding as you keep reinvesting your monthly savings and paper profits in the market as well as possibly your employer's matching funds.

Eventually, however, your time for accumulation begins to narrow. Your ability to accept risk begins to diminish as you approach retirement. When does this start to happen? It's different for different people, but around the time you turn 50 – 55 years old is the time to begin shifting your strategy. You don't want to drop your nest egg just before you need it.

Besides, the effect of dollar-cost averaging is nearly zero in the last few years of your accumulation because when the market declines you will lose much more than you make by buying the small number of shares with your monthly investment. Buying a few shares at a discount that late in the game is like putting an eyedropper's worth of water in the ocean. It makes no tangible difference. The effect of your entire account going down far outweighs the effect of buying a few shares at a lower price. Your dollar-cost averaging days are pretty much over as you near retirement because preservation, not accumulation, is the name of the new game.

Someplace along the way, you must decide how much and when to begin to preserve some of your accumulated wealth, and a great way to do this is to simply ask the question, "How much of my retirement funds can I afford to lose?" Chances are you don't want to lose any!

Another way to gauge the right time to begin shifting your investments into preservation is this old rule of thumb: 100 minus your age is the most you should have at risk. Even so, at age 65, having 35% of your funds vulnerable to loss may still be too much if you think that the markets are at all-time highs.

What I've noticed is that everyone who walks into my office nowadays has almost ALL of their money at risk…it's all in the market. I might agree with that when the market is going up, and the trend is your friend…except the second part of that favorite expression is that the trend is your friend *until the end*…and no one can predict the end accurately.

> "The market can remain irrational much longer than your account can last."
>
> **John Maynard Keynes**

If anything, the end of the upswing may come suddenly and drop your wealth by 20% or more, leaving you high, dry and remorseful without enough time (5 years? 10 years?) to get back to par. Is that what you want to happen? Of course not.

Here's an analogy. Do you own a house? Yes. Did you insure your house? Of course. Do you have fire insurance on it? Of course. What's the probability that your house will burn down? I don't know for sure. About 1 in 1,000 is what I've read, yet you still have fire insurance on your house.

Would it be a true statement to say you would *probably* have more money if you stopped buying fire insurance? Yes, that's a true statement. It would also be really stupid, right?

But why? Not because of the probability of a house fire, but because of the devastating consequences. This brings up the topic of risk management. How do you conduct good risk management in any area of your life?

First, you look at the consequences; then you let the probability determine your cost to protect it.

It's the same thing with everyone's house…they all have fire insurance. If someone said you'd probably have more money if you didn't buy fire insurance, you'd probably cover your ears and run away, as well you should.

Logically, the next questions to pop up are, "Does anybody have any money in retirement accounts? Do you have any kind of protection on that?" Most likely your retirement account is much bigger than your house…so is there more than a 1 in 1,000 chance that your retirement funds could "burn down," at least part way?

Of course.

Probably the biggest industry in America is the insurance industry with all of us insuring each other for all the risks we have to accept…yet for our biggest asset, the asset that is supposed to protect our lifestyle through the last 20 – 30 years of our lives; people do nothing to protect it.

Smiling Retirees know this is madness!

Mistake #2: Having all your money in one asset category.

Almost all the liquid money in the United States is pretty much in only one asset category right now…mutual funds in retirement accounts. There are other asset categories, you know! The other asset classes are bonds, real estate, cash in all its various forms, and commodities.

If you have all your assets in a single category, you're asking for trouble if anything bad happens to it. This is really putting all your nest eggs in one basket!

There are about a dozen giant institutions that own billions of dollars of stock from huge corporations like Walgreens, McDonald's, 3M, Johnson & Johnson… When the fund managers start dumping their stock holdings, who's going to buy them?

There are no buyers because everyone sees everyone else selling, and they don't want to buy the stock while it's on its way down. The market makers want to get out, too, but since they have to make a market, they will price everything, so they have less chance of losing. That means you'll have to ride the elevator to the proverbial bottom. You can't unload your stock because no one is buying until the stock settles somewhere south of where the selling began.

It sounds easy. "Just sell it!", But it doesn't work like that in the real world when the markets are in chaos. Small investors are usually the last ones to know about a sudden sea-change, and that's why the axiom that the small investors buy at the top and sell at the bottom is typically so true. The mistake they make is having all their money in only one asset category.

If you want to sleep well at night, asset allocation is critical for wealth preservation!

Most investors don't do their due diligence and study investment theory or have enough market experience to truly know a good or bad risk when they see it. Asset allocation is not investing in different categories of stocks. Asset allocation is investing in several of the other asset categories. The reason this is a great idea and should be part of your portfolio and investment strategy is that the five categories are not correlated with each other, so when one category slows down or reverses, another category usually accelerates and increases. The real estate market is different from the commodities market which is different from the stock markets which is different from the bond markets which is different from the cash markets.

If you have all your money in one of those categories, you are at risk for that market. It's called *systematic risk*, or risk if the whole system goes down. Each category has its own set of benefits and detractions, too. You shouldn't have too much of your wealth in only real estate, for example, because real estate isn't very liquid; it can be difficult to sell if you needed your money rather quickly. On the other hand, of course, if the property is producing income, this can be a benefit worth choosing as it is an important part of your financial portfolio.

To reiterate the key point, if you put all your assets in one category, you're at a much higher level of risk, and one that you shouldn't have to have since you have choices, and retiring you have less time to recover. There is already enough risk when investing. Why add to it?

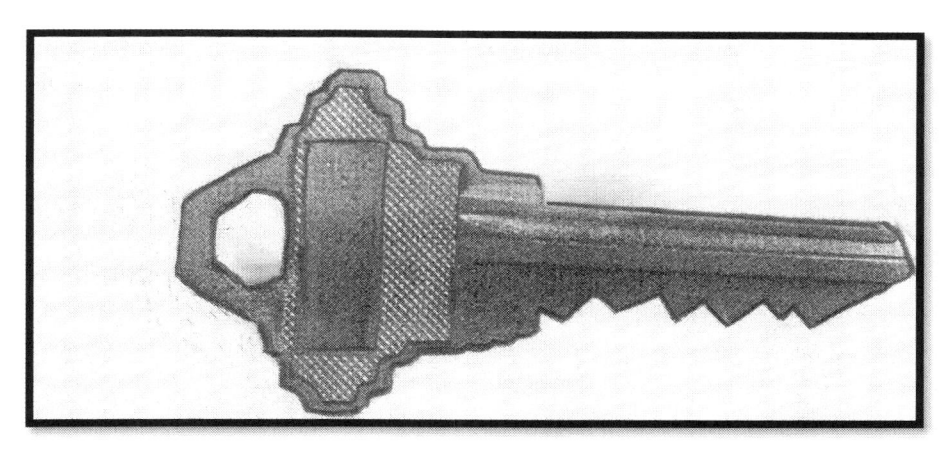

Find a financial advisor who can do the calculations that show you how these correlations work so you can spread your risk among the different asset categories. Ideally, you want to have your assets in a variety of categories, so they work together to give you a chance for the best outcomes in the limited amount of time you have to secure your retirement's future.

Even so, if I lined up 1,000 people and I asked them about their risk management strategy, most people will not have one, and those that do will tell me that their risk management strategy is diversification. When I quiz them on that, they tell me they're diversified because they have different mutual funds! If they're a more sophisticated investor, and this will only be 2 or 3 out of 1,000, I'll hear them say, "Well, I have money in large-cap stocks, I have money in small-cap growth, emerging markets, and technology," but what they don't realize is that it's all in the stock market…which is just one asset class.

When the stock market goes down, it's usually all going down together…and their wealth with it. As time goes by, people tend to forget about the last big decline and become more complacent. They figure that the markets will come back because they always do. But in retirement, they are usually withdrawing money, not adding money to their accounts…an extreme difference.

The truth is that all investments are the same in the sense that they are all worth the present value of the future income. All you have to do is get a good idea of what the future income will be, put that into your financial calculator with a discount rate, (you can use the corresponding US Treasury rate), select a time span, get a value, and buy it if it is selling at a sufficient margin of safety. Smiling Retirees know if they can't get a pretty good idea of the future income, they don't buy it.

> "People should arrange their affairs so that they are OK if the market were to shut down for 10 years."
>
> Warren Buffet
>
> (He is not predicting this: He is only talking about not having to rely on withdrawing money at an inopportune time.)

Mistake #3: Relying on statistics or market returns to manage your retirement funds.

Using statistics to manage your investments is foolishness.

If your head is in the oven and your feet are in the freezer, on average you're okay, right? Yet, how much sense does that make?

Most of the money poured into the market was at the beginning of 2000 and the end of 2007, right before two the biggest market crashes. Uninformed investors reviewed fund and stock statistics and thought they saw an imperative to buy, but instead lost much of their money because statistics can be seriously misleading.

Let's say you read that the market is earning 7%. That's a pretty decent return…but it's specific to a particular period. Fund managers will report their fund's return statistics over 1, 3, 5, and ten-year units (or the life of the fund). Be careful of the life of the fund statistic. It may have started at the bottom of the last decline.

If the 5-year period is from the end of 2008 to 2013, the fund will probably look fantastic, but if instead the fund was measured a year earlier, from the top of 2007 to 2012, it doesn't look so good. The fund will have completely different statistics.

If the fund is measured from 2005 to 2015, it looks fantastic. If it's measured from 2007 to 2017, it may not look so good. In about two years, fund managers will have a field day advertising their fund because the measurement will be from the end of 2008 to the end of 2018 and most likely, unless there is a market crash, the fund will look like it's a high-performing investment…which may not be so.

So what does this tell us? Statistics are misleading because achieving those same high percentage returns means an investor would have had to buy the fund at the beginning of the period. Not only that, but what does it all really mean anyway? Most people didn't have a huge amount of money in the beginning, and never add or take out any money. Instead, they added money every month, month after month, quarter after quarter, year after year, decade after decade. Also, their employers may have matched those additions.

The statistics don't tell us anything about how the fund would have done while adding money, or how it would perform when taking money out, for that matter. And the latter is what is really important in retirement. The funds are all required to report using the same periods so that each manager can't pick the period that shows the fund's best performance. At least the periods must be uniform!

The truth is that when you use a statistical analysis comparing a fund's performance against the market, it's not necessarily pertinent to your particular situation.

This invites a short discussion on the nature of risk. Some would have you believe that risk is volatility, but that's inaccurate.

If I had a stock and it fluctuated between $45 and $55, and I compared it to a stock fluctuating between $30 and $70, which one is more volatile?

The latter one is, of course, because it has much wider fluctuations. So if we just go by the statistics, we would say that one is riskier.

If the price right now is at 30, that theory suggests that it is riskier than the other one that might have a price of 55. That is just plain silly. We'd lose more value if the $55 stock dropped to $45 than if we bought a stock that was already at its lowest value with big upside potential. This, of course, is not guaranteed, and can suddenly go down, but I think you get the point that volatility alone isn't that great a measure of risk.

The volatility is greater, but the risk isn't greater, so just the fact that it's more volatile doesn't mean it has more risk. In fact, at a low point, the more volatile one may be better. *Smiling Retirees* know to look past the statistics and analyze each opportunity based on its merits, not generic statements taken as guiding principles.

The idea of using volatility as a measure of risk really comes from the bell curve. Without getting too far into the weeds, just know that the concept of the bell curve was developed by a famous German mathematician, Carl Friedrich Gauss. He was so famous that Napoleon had his army march around Gauss's hometown on its way to invade Russia.

Gauss noticed that you can always get the average of a bunch of numbers by simply adding them all up and then dividing by how many numbers there are. But when you take the average of 45, 50, and 55, you'll get the same average if you used these three numbers: 1 million, 150 and negative 1 million. The answer for both sets of numbers is 50. Mathematically that's all well and good…but it's a different experience if your account is worth a million one day and minus a million the next. The variance is much different.

He called his calculation the standard error. We now call it the standard deviation. The question is, "Does it say anything about the future?" Gauss said that you could use this calculation for future predictions if two factors are true. One, each event has to be independent of each other. Like flipping a coin. Each flip is independent of the one before it. And two, each event has to be the same size like one head or one tail.

Is this true in investing? No. If stocks start running up or down, the changes are not always the same size. Sometimes they gap up or down, and they are certainly not independent. Everybody is watching, and if a stock starts falling, other people may also start selling. So, using these methods to predict the future of investments is simply not reliable. What you will find in the real world is that the tails on the bell curve are much fatter than the calculations predict.

Don't get me wrong. I am not saying I don't put the numbers into your spreadsheets. I do. What I am saying is, don't expect them to be predictive of what happens next.

A better measurement of risk is probably to look at the history of the stock or fund and find its maximum draw-down.

This is what I think Warren Buffett would say. It's nonsense to say a fund, or stock, has more risk because it's more volatile. It depends on the price.

People look at their 401(k)s and wonder which funds to include. Of course, we know that past performance is not an indication of future performance. Smiling Retirees remember that conditions change over time, and just because one stock or index is doing well today may not have any bearing on how well or poorly it will do later.

If you are going to be an active market investor, you just can't "set and forget" your portfolio's investments. You must pay attention. There is a whole lot of extra work investors must do if they are serious and want to compete against the market makers. Set and forget is for a slow cooker, not an investment practice. There is a myth about professional athletes that they can change professions and become great at another sport. This rarely happens.

The same is true of investment management and other complex endeavors.

Of course, you could always allocate some of your money to guaranteed income and more secure savings and non-correlated investment vehicles.

I'm always astonished to learn what I didn't know I didn't know…and the more I learn, the less I know that I know… If this is true for you, Smiling Retirees know that now could be a good time to work with a financial specialist who can guide them into and through the financial years that lie ahead.

"I THINK YOU SHOULD BE MORE EXPLICIT HERE IN STEP TWO."

Mistake #4: Relying on withdrawals from your retirement accounts to fund your retirement.

A horrible idea. Horrible! Unless you have a lot of money…many millions.

If you do this, you're practicing dollar-cost averaging in reverse.

This is not income. Income is wages, profits, rents, royalties, dividends, interest, pensions, and social security.

Here's an idea to consider. **If something has to move for you to make money, I define that as speculative.**

If you're relying on something going up to replace the value of a resource you used up, you're playing a dangerous game. Think of the farmer selling off part of his property. He has 40 acres on the edge of town, and he sells off an acre or two to someone to build a house. The value goes up, and he sells off a few more acres. The value goes up again.

Eventually, he doesn't have any land left. The farmer has been relying on withdrawals, hoping the balance will continually go back up and restore the original value, but when the market goes down, he's suddenly broke. He has sold off all his land. This is what frequently happens to people in retirement without proper planning.

So how do you plan for retirement? I ask the people in my

classes if they've gone online and used those online calculators. Most have. They input their age and when they want to retire and how much money they have, how much income they'll need, and how much they think their accounts will earn. Well, where do they get the rate of return? Let's say a person inputs 6%. Does that mean someone's going to drop 6% into their pot of money every year?

No. it simply means that if you didn't add or take out any money, over some time your account would have produced that return. But in retirement, you are taking out money. Some years the return is negative, and when the accounts go down, and you are withdrawing money, they go down faster.

These online "tools" are not based in reality but only on wishful thinking. Planning for retirement is a lot more complicated than planning to live off your accumulated wealth by selling off your assets. Once you start selling them, it may be only a matter of time until they're gone, and that may occur while you still need the money. What you may want to do is arrange for some guaranteed income from part of your retirement funds. Added to social security, this will give you a base from which you can invest the balance of your wealth to help offset rising costs and taxes.

With continually rising inflation, the potential for increased taxes, extended life spans, and exorbitant health care costs, planning for retirement is a serious business, and you should see a qualified financial advisor while there's still time, so you can be sure to be a *Smiling Retiree.*

> "The income tax has made liars out of more Americans than golf."
>
> Will Rogers

Mistake #5: Not taking income taxes into account.

The biggest expense in your life will probably be income taxes. A possible exception could be health care expenses. Income taxes still will be huge. If you are a great investor and make all kinds of return on your investment but ignore income taxes, you will not do well overall. Most of the money right now in America is in the Baby Boomers retirement accounts, some $24,000,000,000,000 ($24 trillion) as I write this.

All your life it has paid to put money into your retirement accounts and get the deduction, and later when you take the money out, it has been at a lower tax bracket. Now tax rates have turned the corner and are going up.

We must take taxes into account. I have outlined strategies in this book to try to get your funds into the tax-advantaged or tax-free category. ***Smiling Retirees*** take a careful look at doing so.

Mistake #6: Not taking inflation into account.

By inflation, I am not talking about the official inflation rate published by the government. I am talking about your own personal rise in costs over the length of your retirement.

How much will that rise be? I don't know. And neither does anyone else.

If history is any guide, costs will continue to go up over time. I can't find a case in history where a country has not devalued its currency. You can go back and look at the gold content in Roman coins and see the decline in gold, and the rise in the lead over the years. The same goes for the British Pound and every other currency I can think of.

Ours seems to be no different.

If we depend only on a fixed income for our retirement, we will probably end up with very little purchasing power left. It would be prudent to mix into our investment portfolio some ways to keep up with rising costs. Stocks have kept up over the long haul, but not while inflation was high. If you look at stock prices in the '70s, the last time there was raging inflation in the US, stocks were terrible. That's if you owned them at the beginning of the raging inflation, starting around 1965. Some of them were good to buy, though, when they got cheap enough.

In fact, marketing advisors told us in the early '80s to never use the words "the market" because people had been losing money for so long. After inflation ended and started coming down in the early '80s along with interest rates, stocks recovered, but they did poorly while inflation was high.

Smiling Retirees don't bet on their stocks keeping up with inflation until the cycle ends. They look at other ways of acquiring increasing income such as real estate or guaranteed income accounts that have an inflation hedge built in.

Mistake #7: Not taking rising interest rates into account.

The third of the three coming tidal waves…

Interest rates are almost certain to go up in the future. No rational person would loan out their money for 30 years by buying a 30-year Treasury bond to lock in 2.2% interest. You might get one of these bonds for the guarantee of the federal government, but for sure not to lock in the interest rate. Interest rates are near the lowest in anyone's lifetime and are unsustainable.

When will rates go up.? I don't know, and neither does anyone else, but we better factor in the near certainty in your retirement plans. It might sound good that interest rates will probably go up so you might actually make some money on your savings accounts, but remember, inflation generally goes hand in hand with interest rates. So does taxation. The truth is that the 15% interest rates that people fondly remember from their CDs in the early '80s actually ended up giving you less after taxes and inflation than you are earning now.

The other effect of rising interest rates, of course, will be a drag on the economy. Companies will have to pay higher costs to expand, and builders will have to pay higher costs to borrow money to build, as will the purchasers of those properties. Car buyers will have to pay more. Perhaps most importantly, the government at every level will have to pay more to refinance all the bonds as they come due.

Smiling Retirees know we are entering the next phase of the economy when interest rates, inflation, and taxes all go up. Watch out below!

Mistake #8: Ignoring the Buffet rule: Don't lose money.

Not so important when you first start out. Vitally important when you approach retirement.

If your retirement account drops in half, you have to make 100% on it to get back to even. How many years could that take? This is very hard to do, and you lose too much time, one of your chief resources.

You recovered from the last two big declines, but now you are closer to, or in, retirement, and you probably will be withdrawing money, not adding money to your retirement accounts.

We talked about *REVERSE* dollar-cost averaging. *Smiling Retirees* know this danger is very real and can make your accounts decline even faster.

> "$100 placed at 7% interest compounded quarterly for 200 years will increase to more than $100,000,000--by which time it will be worth nothing."
>
> Robert Heinlein
> (And if it is taxed at 30% every year, it will be worth even less.
> Navi Dowty)

Navi J. Dowty CFA®

Mistake #9: Not taking the sequence of returns into account.

If you don't add money or take any out of your accounts, will they be worth more or less if all of the "down" years are at the beginning of your investing period?

Frequently people say less. Actually, it is exactly the same, but when you are withdrawing from your accounts, if large down years are at the beginning, you probably will run out of money. This is really amazing because if you put all the positive years in the beginning and withdraw money over time, your account will grow even if you factor in inflation.

Reverse the time when the negative years occur, and you run out of money. Both scenarios have the same average returns. Smiling Retirees know that the average return is pretty meaningless.

> "Money Can't Buy You Happiness. Poverty isn't so great at it either."
>
> Navi Dowty

Mistake #10: Not taking the sequence of withdrawals into account.

Under many circumstances, this can have an even bigger effect on your accounts than the sequence of returns.

Should you take money out of your IRAs first, or your taxable accounts, or your Roth IRAs, or your 401(k)s or Roth 403(b)s?

Should you start your Social Security yet? Or should you delay taking it and let it grow by 8% per year? In some cases, you can end up with twice as much money by optimizing the sequence of withdrawal when you take money from different types of accounts.

I have seen this one strategy alone make the difference of people running out of money or having a sufficient amount for their lifetime with money left over at the end to leave to their heirs. I can't give you a rule of thumb because, like many tips in this book, it requires a calculation specific to your unique situation.

Except one. You should probably leave the tax-free money until the end, assuming that David Walker is right and taxes have to double. Smiling Retirees are keenly aware of where they withdraw funds because the sequence of withdrawal may have a huge impact on their wealth.

Mistake #11: Not using charitable strategies.

I see many people planning to leave some money to charity after they are gone. They usually want to leave some to the kids, sometimes all of it.

You could be getting a current tax deduction for that future gift to charity and at the same time increasing your income. If you arrange things just right, you can still leave the same amount or more to your heirs…maybe even tax-free.

If you have a highly appreciated stock or piece of real estate that isn't giving you much income right now, you can put it into a properly designed trust with your favorite charity as the remainder interest, sell it without paying any current income tax, and increase your income dramatically. You may even get a current tax deduction to further increase your income.

Smiling Retirees know if they use this strategy, they will have to leave some of it to charity eventually, but frequently they can replace the value of the asset for their heirs as well. Besides, helping out your favorite cause is gratifying.

Mistake #12: Judging items by their name rather than by what they actually do.

Take the word "trust" for example. People assume they know what a trust is because it has the word 'trust' in it. Taking a mental shortcut and assuming what financial instruments do based on their label only breeds inaccuracy, misdirection, or lost opportunities. There are numerous kinds of trusts. They are very flexible and range from simple revocable living trusts that really only avoid probate to very complex arrangements that help preserve assets under many different scenarios.

When people think in terms of shortcuts based on the name of a financial product, they usually do themselves a disservice. The container doesn't mean anything; it's what's inside that counts. Not all pizzas are the same; they don't all come with pepperoni and olives. If you say you have a pet at home, this really doesn't describe anything. Your pet might be a goldfish or a mountain lion.

Here is an example of the inherent confusion. If I say I'm in a money market fund, what does that mean? Most people know a money market fund is a low-risk cash investment instrument...but is it guaranteed?

If it's at a bank, it's FDIC-insured and guaranteed up to the FDIC limit, but if it's a money market mutual fund, it's not necessarily insured. It's probably pretty stable, but it's not guaranteed by the FDIC. Same words, but very different investments. This is an example of a label that does not properly describe the underlying product.

Take a look at reverse mortgages. Lots of people have heard negative information about reverse mortgages without ever investigating them, yet reverse mortgages are actually a brilliant tool when applied to circumstances where they are effective. They're not right for everybody, but they may have a place in your tool chest, should you need one, and particularly at these historically low-interest rates. Like everything else, it's a calculation to see what works best for you.

Another classic case is the term, "fixed income asset." Sounds pretty safe, right?

What fixed income usually refers to is bonds. As we have seen, bonds sometimes lose money if they default or interest rates go up. What is fixed in a fixed income asset is the *income*, not the *principal*.

"Annuity" is another example, in fact probably the biggest example. If I said, "I have an annuity," what would you say? You might reply it means I have payments coming to me periodically throughout my life based on the principal held by an insurance company. Yet, this is only one example of an annuity. Your pension is an annuity. In fact, all state lotteries are annuities.

There are really three kinds of annuities: immediate annuities, fixed annuities, and variable annuities. A variable annuity is nothing more than a set of mutual funds within an annuity wrapper, so your principal and your earnings are at risk. There are also fixed annuities similar to CDs but which are not federally insured; the principal is guaranteed by the insurance company. You may get a fixed interest rate, but the interest earnings could also be linked to a market index; the earnings will vary while the principal stays secure.

It's clear that when it comes to the word "annuity," you don't really know what the word means unless you look at the details; an "annuity" can be any type of annuity.

Perhaps most egregious are the articles trying to make a pitch for or against one investment category or another. Look in the back of a magazine, or watch the ads the media outlet is promoting. If they are for banks, the product is probably going to be some type of bank account. If they are for stocks, the ad will be for mutual funds. If you go to a Ford dealer, for example, the offer is probably going to be a Ford, not a Chevy.

A lot of time the articles will confuse and merge together the traits of different assets under a particular broad name like annuities. What they say is that you lose flexibility, lose your money if you die, and have high fees. They have selected ***characteristics*** of different categories of annuities.

Immediate annuities give you income for life. They are inflexible. Variable annuities usually have high fees, but give you a chance to get market-based gains and losses. Fixed annuities have guaranteed principal. The articles merge the negative traits of all these different types of annuities together and make it seem that putting money into an annuity will give you all of the negatives, which is not true. Each type has its own pros and cons.

It's better to think about what you're trying to accomplish first, and then be open-minded to learning more about what's available to accomplish what you need, no matter what the words sound like. And of course, you need to read the risk disclosure documents that will come with all of the different types of savings vehicles and investments. Smiling Retirees understand that words seldom accurately describe the underlying tool, and they take the time to investigate a little deeper.

Mistake #13: Confusing correlation with causation.

I think we do this naturally as human beings. When we're looking at two things, we tend to confuse what's actually happening.

If you go to a building burning down, you will probably see firemen there. Firemen are usually correlated with burning buildings. That doesn't mean that firemen cause burning buildings.

What would be a classic case? We say that rising interest rates make bond prices lower, but actually the opposite is what is really happening. Rising bond prices cause long-term interest rates to go down. The Federal Reserve directly controls the short-term interest rates, but the bond market controls the long-term interest rates. Sometimes people are unwilling to buy bonds at the offered price, and that causes the price of bonds to drop, making interest rates go up.

A bond is a financial instrument that allows you to lock in an interest rate. So the question is, do you want to lock in the offered interest rate? Are you happy with the amount of interest you'll receive for the duration of the term? You'd probably lose a lot of money buying a 30-year bond right now if you had to sell it in the next few years, should interest rates go up. When interest rates go up, the value of the bond will go down.

People sometimes think bonds are a safe haven from stocks. I've heard people say, "Well, I'll just switch to bonds." For over 35 years, declining bond interest and rising bond prices have worked opposite from stocks. Now, however, bond prices have gone up, and so have stocks, so they have been pretty well correlated. The next phase of the cycle is just the opposite, though. Rising interest rates will make both stocks and bonds go down. The opposite will be true if interest rates keep going down, of course. Do you think they will?

Here is another example. People tend to change financial advisors after a big market crash. The new advisor puts you into his favorite investments right at the bottom. He then looks like a hero. He is correlated with you recovering your money if the markets go back up. You tend to blame the old guy and make a new *set point* in your thinking starting from the low point. We do the same with political figures, phases of the moon, the weather, and any number of other events that seem to be correlated to our fortunes…but do these events really cause our rising or falling fortunes? Not necessarily.

The *Smiling Retiree* makes no assumptions and looks carefully at what's happening, discerning correlation from causation before investing.

> "We simply try to be brave when other people are fearful, and fearful when other people are brave."
>
> **Warren Buffet**

Navi J. Dowty CFA®

Mistake #14: Not evaluating "What if I'm wrong?"

If we want to learn the great truths of life, we can look to the philosophers… like William Shakespeare. Yes, he has a lot of philosophy in his plays. In his play, Julius Caesar, Cassius says to Brutus, *"The fault, dear Brutus, is not in our stars, but in ourselves…"* That's pretty good. Sometimes we can be our own worst enemy.

> I kind of like the way that great American philosopher, Pogo said it,
>
> "We have met the enemy and he is us."

Nobody seems to do this. What if you're wrong? You have to stress-test your portfolio.

You have to evaluate, "If I'm wrong, what happens to my precious retirement money?"

What if I'm wrong about tax rates going up? How can that hurt me? How about inflation?

What if I'm wrong about interest rates going up? What if they go down? How can I protect myself if the market does things contrary to my planning and expectations?

What unforeseen black swan events could happen? How am I positioned to either maintain my wealth, preserve my wealth, or increase my wealth and income?

Could there be rising costs in retirement? Almost certainly.

If your head is in the oven and your feet are in the freezer, on average you're okay, right? Yet, how much sense does that make?

The *Smiling Retiree* never enters a position without considering what can go wrong, planning how to protect the wealth in the position, and planning how to get out of the position should the wealth become jeopardized.

If you're wrong and something bad happens, will you stand by and watch your wealth evaporate…or will you have an action plan ready to execute?

Have a plan! Don't freeze at the controls and crash into the mountain…and don't hope that someone will get you out of the market. It's up to you to make the proper allocations at the beginning, not the fund manager. They are focused on managing their fund and trying to outperform their benchmark. Your job is to allocate how much to put into each category.

I ask people all the time did you sell at the bottom and get out last time? They say no. Why not? They say, "I don't want to take the loss." How about at the top? They tell me, "I can't sell then, either, because the account is doing so well." So…if you can't sell at the bottom, and you can't sell at the top, you are just in the market and subject to all its whims. It's better, then, to allocate the proper amounts for your situation.

Smiling Retirees always know what they are going to do if the worst starts to happen, and they are ready to do it!

APPENDIX

We have a new tax law starting in 2018. It was really a suspension for most of the changes and will revert back to the old rules on January 1, 2026

This new tax law reduced the amount of the deduction you can have for state and local taxes to $10,000 per year. This limitation is not a big deal for people that live in rural areas and don't have a lot of property taxes.

However, if you live in New York, Chicago, San Francisco, or other high property tax areas, this is going to be a very, very big hit. I looked at many tax returns last year where the people had $65,000, $75,000, $85,000, $110,000 or more in itemized deductions and they're not going to be able to itemize anymore at all. This loss of deductions will be a very big tax burden to them.

Let's summarize the things that we've lost. We lost a lot of deductions from state and local property taxes. Like I say, down to $10,000.

You still have medical deductions. Anything above ten percent of your adjusted gross income can be a deduction.

You can still have interest deductions on your primary residence and a second house. The loans have to be secured on those houses separately, and they can't exceed a million dollars if you want to deduct the interest.

Can you borrow money on your principal residence to buy the second home and deduct the interest?

Not, anymore.

We also lost all the miscellaneous itemized deductions, such as tax prep fees, investment management fees, unreimbursed employee business expenses, moving expense deductions, and casualty losses. You can't deduct casualty losses unless they are from a federally designated disaster area.

Employees that spend a lot of money buying things for their jobs and employees that drive their personal cars for work will not get to deduct those expenses anymore.

Here's another change.

For a while back in the seventies and early eighties, you could put properties in your children's name and take advantage of the fact that the kids were not in a high tax bracket.

Then Congress got wise to that ploy and started taxing minor children's passive income at the parent's tax rate.

The new tax law does away with that. Now the rule is simplified. You no longer have to tax the kids at the parent's tax rate. The kids will be taxed at the trust rates.

The highest rates.

If their passive income gets above $12,000, then we're talking about the maximum rate, which is 37 percent. So, simplification does not always equal savings.

If we're not talking about too much income, it's still possible to benefit. If you are only talking about a few thousand dollars, you can still shift some to the kids and possibly benefit. It's a calculation just like everything else in this book.

Entertainment is out as a deduction.

Losing the entertainment deduction will be a very big deal for many businesses.

So, if you have your own business and you used to take clients to a golf outing, that's no longer available to deduct for small businesses and corporations alike.

What was not taken away is gifts.

Rather than taking somebody golfing, you may want to give them a ticket for green fees, because gifts are still able to be deducted if they are appropriate, necessary, and customary for your business.

The new big benefit for businesses is a reduction in taxes.

So, if you're operating your business as a C Corporation, they lowered the maximum tax rate from 35 percent to 21 percent.

That's a pretty big reduction.

What about all the other businesses?

Most businesses in America are small businesses. Most small businesses in America are sole proprietorships. The sole proprietorship also gets a deduction; although, it's a little funky.

The sole proprietor's deduction comes off as a reduction on their personal tax return.

What am I talking about? Most small businesses file their business taxes on their schedule C.

Whatever the net income from that business is, it is reduced by a 20 percent deduction just above their taxable income line.

The same is true if you operate as an S Corp or an LLC.

However, this deduction doesn't show up at all on your company tax return.

Income from your own business will show up on your schedule C, or if it's an S Corp or an LLC, it'll show up on line 4b. These are called pass-through entities.

But then, just above the taxable income on line 9, you'll get to take off 20 percent if your total income is under the 5th tax bracket, which in 2019 starts at $321,451.

It is indexed for inflation, so when you read this, the number may be different, but the concept is the same.

If your income is above $321,400, it phases out over the next hundred thousand dollars.

And when your personal income hits $421,400, you don't get any deduction at all for your small business.

Unless your business is architecture or engineering. Why architecture and engineering? I guess they just liked architects and engineers.

This is a pretty big anomaly because you could have two people that own a business. One of them gets the 20 percent reduction, and the other one who has too much income doesn't get the 20 percent reduction.

Because the deduction of 20 percent occurs after your adjusted gross income is calculated, the business income still affects taxation on your social security distributions.

So, let's talk about that for a second.

You may wonder, are your social security benefits going to be taxed if you're taking social security and you are still running your business?

Social Security is tax-free up to a provisional income of $32,000 for a couple, at which time 50 percent of it is taxed.

And then at $44,000, 85 percent of it starts to get taxed.

The thresholds are $25,000 and $34,000 for single taxpayers.

That provisional income is determined by taking half of your social security payments, and then adding to that, your modified adjusted gross income. Modified meaning that you take your adjusted gross income, and add back any tax-free municipal bond interest, and deductions you had such as IRA'S.

The effect is that you don't get a deduction for the qualified business income, QBI, to reduce taxes on your social security. That deduction comes off after the calculation of your social security tax.

So, to make the long story short, we won some, and we lost some.

And where you end-up really depends on your characteristic, income, and deductions that occur on each line of the tax return.

Each one of those lines is a choice that you've made. And if you've made a choice, you can unmake that choice and change it for the future if it benefits you.

> Worried about an IRS audit? Avoid what's called a red flag. That's something the IRS always looks for. For example, say you have some money left in your bank account after paying taxes. That's a red flag.
>
> --Jay Leno

Since everybody is different, you need to get with your tax planner today to figure out how to optimize your tax situation.

This is just a slight smattering of some of the new tax rules. The important thing is how to think about your taxes. Everything about your taxes truly is in your control.

There are rules, and then there are strategies to utilize those rules and combine them in a manner that is most beneficial for you.

I always ask my students if they have a five-year-old child or grandchild. If not, I ask them if they ever were a 5-year-old child. That pretty well covers everybody. Then I ask, could you teach the 5-year-old the moves on a chess board? The pawn moves forward one space, the bishop moves on the diagonals, etc.

And of course, the answer is yes; you could teach a 5-year-old the basic moves of the chess pieces. Could the 5-year-old put the moves together and beat a world chess champion though? Almost certainly not. It is the planning ahead and the interaction of the different strategies that are most important.

Your taxes are like that as well. How do you put all the myriad rules and opportunities together to end up with the optimal plan for you?

That is the question I attempt to answer for you with the *Smiling Retiree Process.*

2019 Tax Rates

These will change every year

Taxable Income

Single

0 to $9,700	10 %
$9,701 to $39,475	12 %
$39,476 to $84,200	22 %
$84,201 to $$160,725	24 %
$160,726 10 $204,100	32 %
$204,101 to $510,300	34 %
Over $510,300	37%

Married Filing Jointly

0 to $19,400	10%
$19,401 to $ $78,950	12%
$78,951 to $168,400	22%
$168,401 to $321,450	24%
$321,451 to $408,200	32%
$408,201 to $612,350	34%
Over $612,350	37%

[Image of IRS Form 1040, U.S. Individual Income Tax Return, 2018]

> A fine is a tax for doing something wrong.
> A tax is a fine for doing something right.

Form 1040 (2018)						Page 2

	1	Wages, salaries, tips, etc. Attach Form(s) W-2			1	
Attach Form(s) W-2. Also attach Form(s) W-2G and 1099-R if tax was withheld.	2a	Tax-exempt interest	2a	b Taxable interest	2b	
	3a	Qualified dividends	3a	b Ordinary dividends	3b	
	4a	IRAs, pensions, and annuities	4a	b Taxable amount	4b	
	5a	Social security benefits	5a	b Taxable amount	5b	
	6	Total income. Add lines 1 through 5. Add any amount from Schedule 1, line 22			6	
	7	Adjusted gross income. If you have no adjustments to income, enter the amount from line 6; otherwise, subtract Schedule 1, line 36, from line 6			7	
Standard Deduction for— • Single or married filing separately, $12,000 • Married filing jointly or Qualifying widow(er), $24,000 • Head of household, $18,000 • If you checked any box under Standard deduction, see instructions.	8	Standard deduction or itemized deductions (from Schedule A)			8	
	9	Qualified business income deduction (see instructions)			9	
	10	Taxable income. Subtract lines 8 and 9 from line 7. If zero or less, enter -0-			10	
	11	a Tax (see inst.) _____ (check if any from: 1 ☐ Form(s) 8814 2 ☐ Form 4972 3 ☐ _____) b Add any amount from Schedule 2 and check here ▶ ☐			11	
	12	a Child tax credit/credit for other dependents _____ b Add any amount from Schedule 3 and check here ▶ ☐			12	
	13	Subtract line 12 from line 11. If zero or less, enter -0-			13	
	14	Other taxes. Attach Schedule 4			14	
	15	Total tax. Add lines 13 and 14			15	
	16	Federal income tax withheld from Forms W-2 and 1099			16	
	17	Refundable credits: a EIC (see inst) _____ b Sch. 8812 _____ c Form 8863 _____ Add any amount from Schedule 5 _____			17	
	18	Add lines 16 and 17. These are your total payments			18	
Refund	19	If line 18 is more than line 15, subtract line 15 from line 18. This is the amount you overpaid			19	
	20a	Amount of line 19 you want refunded to you. If Form 8888 is attached, check here ▶ ☐			20a	
Direct deposit? See instructions.	▶ b	Routing number _____ ▶ c Type: ☐ Checking ☐ Savings				
	▶ d	Account number _____				
	21	Amount of line 19 you want applied to your 2019 estimated tax ▶ 21 _____				
Amount You Owe	22	Amount you owe. Subtract line 18 from line 15. For details on how to pay, see instructions ▶			22	
	23	Estimated tax penalty (see instructions) ▶ 23 _____				

Go to www.irs.gov/Form1040 for instructions and the latest information.

Form **1040** (2018)

Afterword

Special Offer for You

People often ask me, "Hey, Navi, what should I do next?"

The answer is, "I don't know…what does "next" mean for you?"

The only way to know what it means for you is to have a conversation with a specialist, which is why we offer the **Retiree Confidential Opportunity Conversation.**

It's a great opportunity for you, and here are my three promises:

Number One: There won't be anything for you to buy.

Number Two: I'm usually going to be able to uncover at least two opportunities to either increase your income or reduce your taxes.

Number Three: You will know what to do next if anything.

If you would like to schedule yours, **give me a call at** 630893-4142 **or** 715-845-4367.

I'd love to speak with you.

Check for updates at -   www.NaviDowty.com

Made in the USA
Columbia, SC
09 March 2019